closer

closer

MUSINGS ON INTIMACY, MARRIAGE, & GOD

VALERIE SCHULTZ

ave maria press AmP notre dame, indiana

Parts of this book appeared previously as short essays in *America*, *Human Development*, *The Bakersfield Californian*, *St. Anthony Messenger*, and *Mothering*.

Biblical quotations in this book are from the *Catholic Youth Bible*, NRSV, Winona, MN: St. Mary's Press, © 2000. Used by permission. All rights reserved.

© 2008 by Ave Maria Press, Inc.

Founded in 1865, Ave Maria Press is a ministry of the Indiana Province of Holy Cross.

www.avemariapress.com

ISBN-10 1-59471-073-2   ISBN-13 978-1-59471-073-5

Cover and text design by Katherine Robinson Coleman.

Printed and bound in the United States of America.

Library of Congress Cataloging-in-Publication Data

Schultz, Valerie.
Closer : musings on intimacy, marriage, and God / by Valerie Schultz.
                    p. cm.
Includes bibliographical references.
ISBN-13: 978-1-59471-073-5
ISBN-10: 1-59471-073-2
1. Marriage—Religious aspects—Christianity. 2. Marriage—Religious aspects—Catholic Church. I. Title.

    BV835.S367 2008
    248.8'44—dc22

                                        2007048749

Contents

Introduction

Come live with me, and be my love,
And we will all the pleasures prove . . .

CHRISTOPHER MARLOWE

I got you, babe.

SONNY & CHER

The subject of intimacy is one I approach with trepidation, because every time I publish an essay on marriage something happens. Every time the magazine arrives in the mail, my husband and I are fighting. The triumphant presentation of my published words is put on hold as I realize that whatever neatly packed wisdom I have written about the sacrament of marriage will seem like a crock to the man to whom I am married, and with whom I'm having less than choice words at that moment. When our issue is resolved, I thank God for the resolution, as well as for the slice of humble pie: It is as though God is reminding me that I am no expert. I may write a good yarn, but I still need God's grace and guidance and love in every stitch and fold of the lovely, frustrating fabric that is marriage.

Imagine my worries about what will happen if I write a whole book.

Nevertheless, after twenty-six years of marriage, I am still an optimist. I believe that the intimacy of marriage is the closest we earthbound humans can come to understanding the intimate way in which our God knows us. I believe that two really do become one, and by the grace of God, the whole really is greater than the sum of the parts. I believe we are like big onions, and as we journey in intimacy, our layers become transparent and are peeled away in the eyes of the one who loves us. Our partner is the only one who knows where some of the layers begin and end, and which ones are false, and which ones are painful when pulled, and which ones are essential to us. In turn we know the same things about our spouse, right down to the inner cloves. With this secret and sacred knowledge comes joy, as well as responsibility.

The sacrament of marriage is a holy partnership. Partners are meant to work together, to complement each other's strengths, to protect each other's vulnerabilities, to mingle vital juices. "If you would marry suitably, marry your equal," said the ancient Roman poet Ovid, around the time of Jesus, and he is still right. Equals who love each other also respect each other. Respect is an essential prerequisite to trust, without which there can be no intimacy.

But equality needn't erect partitions between us. I squirm internally to see a marriage with separate checkbooks: It's as though our individualistic society dictates that in marrying, we cannot dilute one single drop of ourselves without something bad happening. It's marriage by Velcro—no harm, no foul when we decide to rip apart. We'll both still be whole. We haven't sacrificed any precious organ in order to be conjoined. It has the feel of a temporary arrangement, which many marriages, in fact, turn out to be.

When we jettison this thinking, we give and yield and bend. We let go of our isolated wholeness for something more wondrous, if sometimes maddening. Then we two wholes form a new whole: the marriage. Remember those cartoonish Venn diagrams in grade school, which you thought would never have any practical use in real life? Think of a marriage and where the two spousal circles touch, intersect, blend, share. What do we hold in common, and what remains separate? We of course have our own interests, different talents and weaknesses, and maybe even our own check-books: I suppose it can work. But on the things that really matter—there we are shaded as one.

Enter more deeply into the words of St. John: "The word was made flesh and pitched his tent among us" (1:14). These words express the mystery that God, in whom all was creat-ed, has become part of that same creation. . . .

Through the incarnation of God in Jesus Christ all human flesh has been lifted up into God's own intimacy. There is no human being . . . who has not been embraced in and through the flesh of the Word.

The life, death, and resurrection of Jesus manifest to us the full intimacy of this divine embrace.

HENRI M. NOUWEN,
LIFESIGNS

The Incarnation, God in mortal flesh, has always been our most intimate human connection to God. When we consider that God so loved us that Jesus was formed and born of a woman, we understand true intimacy. It is the connection we seek all our lives to share with others. Such a "divine embrace" reassures us that we are loved and valued. And such love teaches us to bring love to every dark corner, to every cold heart, to every unlovable being, to every unforgiving place.

When we experience in our own flesh the intimacy of the Word made flesh, we transcend our fear and our mortality and our doubt. In our intimacy with a loving God, we know for a moment the weightlessness of what we are meant to be, even when our own flesh betrays or fails us. We know what it means to be spiritual beings. We know what it means to pray. We know what it means to put our flesh in the service of things that are not of the flesh, of things that fly beyond the gravity of earth—of the things of God.

And yet we still dare to ponder the mystery of the Incarnation through the maddening, marvelous manifestation of human intimacy. In our earthly marriages, we are challenged to love deeply, beyond our capabilities. This we can do when we rest in God's embrace.

CHAPTER ONE

Mars and Venus, Sitting in a Tree

Helena: Things base and vile, holding no
    quantity,
Love can transpose to form and dignity:
Love looks not with the eyes, but with the
    mind,
And therefore is wing'd Cupid painted blind.
Nor hath love's mind of any judgment taste,
Wings, and no eyes, figure unheedy haste.

WILLIAM SHAKESPEARE,
A MIDSUMMER NIGHT'S DREAM, ACT I, SCENE I

We are creatures of love.

TALKING HEADS

What Does He See in Her?

Our dreams of intimacy, nourished by a romantic culture, often collide with reality. As girls, we are encouraged to imagine the handsome prince scenario: He arrives on a white steed, or at least in a BMW. He is well-dressed, handsome, fit, intelligent, wealthy, powerful. Yet he writes poetry to melt the heart. He knows when to bring flowers, when to make a joke, and when to take charge. He loves only me, and he is a passionate yet considerate lover. He can change a tire as adeptly as he can fold an omelet. Also, he can waltz.

Most of the waltzing I have done is at two in the morning with a two-month-old, and I have to lead.

Seriously, does this sound familiar? By the time we have an inkling that we are looking at the man of our dreams, hopefully we've done some adjusting. We've fine-tuned our expectations. We've figured out what matters, and what is fluff. We have matured. We've also probably been surprised by the intensity of our feelings for a man who is short or bald or nearsighted or allergic or underemployed. We feel a powerful attraction to what we would not have guessed.

We women also would be wise to keep in mind whom our prospective mate has been led to expect by the gorgeous woman scenario: She arrives at his door with cold beer. She is well-endowed, scantily clad, beautiful, fit, reasonably intelligent without being a grind, and smells really good. Yet she is a virgin. She knows when to be quiet, when to make noise, and how to seduce. She loves only him, and she is an attentive and adventurous lover. She can bring home a paycheck as adeptly as she can whip up a home-cooked meal that is heavy on the meat and light on the vegetables. Also, she understands the need for football.

My poor husband snuggles up to a wife who attempts to fill a B-cup and wears socks to bed in the winter.

Men must adjust and mature, too. They come to understand that the woman they desire for life may be flat or odorless or wordy or not blonde or may command a larger salary. And they, too, are surprised when the intensity of their feelings for her knocks them sideways.

Love is often unexplainable.

What makes a marriage work is even more unexplainable. But the quality that is ever present in a good and lasting marriage is intimacy, as well as an awareness of and reliance on the presence of God.

Jesus refers to himself as a bridegroom on several occasions in the gospels. "You cannot make wedding guests fast when the bridegroom is with them, can you?" Jesus asked the sanctimonious Pharisees, who disapproved of the merry behavior of his disciples (Lk 5:34). "The wedding guests cannot mourn as long as the bridegroom is with them, can they? The day will come when the bridegroom is taken away from them, and then they will fast" (Mt 9:15).

John the Baptist tells his disciples about Jesus with these words: "He who has the bride is the bridegroom. The friend of the bridegroom, who stands and hears him, rejoices greatly at the bridegroom's voice. For this reason my joy has been fulfilled. He must increase, but I must decrease" (Jn 3:27–30).

"Were not our hearts burning within us while he was talking to us?" the disciples who traveled the road to Emmaus asked each other (Lk 24:32). After journeying and breaking bread with the risen Jesus, their eyes were opened by an act of tender intimacy. Their words glow with the fervor of one freshly in love, of a lover who longs to spend every moment with the beloved, of a newlywed. We, the Church, are the bride, the perfect match, the lifelong mate chosen by Jesus.

If indeed our relationship with God is like a marriage, then we can see clearly that we choose each other in the same way that God chooses us. As St. Paul tells us in his first letter to the Corinthians, God chooses the foolish, the weak, the lowly and despised, those who count for nothing— that's us. "Not many of you were wise by human standards," he reminds us drily. "Not many of you were powerful, not many were of noble birth" (1 Cor 1:26).

"What does she see in him?" we sometimes wonder about a particular couple. "What does he see in her?" What does God see in us? We may never understand what spark one sees in another, what flame draws one to another, what fire burns in one heart for another. We only know the power of what is there. In our own intimate relationships, we have lived it.

O Lord, you have searched me and known me.
You know when I sit down and when I rise up;
　　you discern my thoughts from far away.
You search out my path and my lying down,
　　and are acquainted with all my ways.
Even before a word is on my tongue,
O Lord, you know it completely. . .
For it was you who formed my inward parts;
　　you knit me together in my mother's womb.
I praise you, for I am fearfully and wonderfully
　　made.
Wonderful are your works;
　　that I know very well.

My frame was not hidden from you,
    when I was being made in secret,
    intricately woven in the depths of the earth.
Your eyes beheld my unformed substance.
In your book were written
    all the days that were formed for me,
    when none of them as yet existed.

Ps 139:1–4, 13–16

Psalm 139, which is often powerfully invoked as a divine argument against abortion, also speaks to our intimacy with God. Here God knows our thoughts and words and deeds outside of time and space; God has intimately formed and knit each and every one of us, and we are indeed "fearfully and wonderfully made" in the image of God. God alone has full power over life and death.

If we believe the poetic words of Psalm 139, that we are all written in God's book, then we understand everything about intimacy. No detail is too small to go unnoticed. There are no secrets. There is an enveloping love and acceptance, and an unbreakable connection to the one we have promised to love.

Men Are From Mars . . .

As much as I believe in the feminist ideals of equal pay for equal work, and equal opportunities, and Title IX for women's sports, and the perfect blending of marital roles, I have to be honest. After over two decades of marriage, I have to admit that men and women really are different.

This was brought home to me, actually brought to my very backyard, at a party for my youngest daughter. In honor of her thirteenth birthday, we invited many boys and girls of various styles and attitudes to come to our home and drink large cups of soda, eat finger foods, and listen to loud music. To please my daughter, there were no games or other party activities planned—and as little visibility of her parents as possible. (Her greatest wish was that we would either become completely invisible or leave the premises, neither of which had any chance of happening, and which is another reason why it *stinks* to be a teenager whose parents pay attention.)

When groups of girls get together, which happens often when four daughters grow up together in one family, they monopolize the phone and the hair appliances, scream and laugh in pitches excruciating to the human ear, wear each other's clothes, and eat a lot. I am used to this pack behavior. But when boys get together, they attack each other. Literally. At my daughter's party, there were clumps of boys in the backyard, wrestling and grabbing and tripping each other. When I emerged to ask that they try not to send each other to the emergency room, they told me they were playing football.

Now, I like football. I watch football. And, Senator, this was *not* football. Although one of them did point to a football lying under a bush nearby as proof of their sport.

My husband advised me to chill out, lest I terminally mortify our daughter, and to let the boys be boys. They're fine, he said. But I wondered, how can he tell?

Eventually the boys entered the house and conversed in coherent sentences with the girls. I can tell you that boys also eat a lot, but not before dipping the wrong foods into the wrong dips and throwing some of their creations at each other. They also seem to be more concerned about their hair than they might want to admit.

The party did end without injury, and without permanent stains, and without the arrival of the police, which made it a successful event for me. Everybody had fun, and the cutest boy did show up, which made it a hit for the birthday girl as well.

But I am left to reflect on the undeniable differences between the sexes, whether innate or acquired. I am thinking these may be obvious to families where sisters and brothers coexist. And even in our lone-male household, there are those scattered moments of crossed communications. Not, of course, that any of the following examples have anything to do with *my* man. I post the large disclaimer that these observations are all hearsay, purely anecdotal, from a friend of a friend, nothing personal. Of course.

© **Men Are From Mars; Women Are From a Place Where There Is Air, and Water, as Well as Carpools and Laundry and Children and Dogs.**

By this I mean that women can multitask. We can make dinner and ponder a work project and do a load of laundry and listen to why our child's science teacher is so totally unfair and figure out the tax versus the delivery charge for an online purchase, all at the same time. Men think they can multitask, but usually the tasks they are managing to juggle are all part of the same task. See if I'm wrong.

© **Men Are From Mars: This Is Why They Act Like Martians.**

Women come home from work and immediately get to work so that they can relax later, if they haven't already fallen asleep. Men come home from work, turn on the TV, and relax on comfortable furniture. Later they are guilt-ridden and haunted by the things they meant to accomplish after work. They also can't figure out why their women are asleep before them so often.

© **Men Are From Mars; Women Say, "Go Home, Already."**

Not really. But when a man says he has gained ten pounds, does he really want his partner to respond with exercise schedules and diet options? Because women do NOT. Women want to hear something like, "You are eternally my goddess and I desire you fantastically." Men possibly want to hear the same thing, leaving out the goddess part. We must all face the fact that we will eventually gain ten pounds, or so. Acceptance and adulation may be what inspires us to finally lose those pounds. Just for each other.

These are egregious generalities—unjust blanket statements, of course. Individual men and women have a vast array of masculine and feminine qualities, all wrapped up in unique human packages. Sometimes men multitask admirably. Sometimes women pursue goals single-mindedly. There may actually be women who leave the toilet seat up, and men who are moved to tears by Hallmark commercials.

Just not usually the ones from earth.

Guess What Dinko Did: A Tale of Two Idiots

An acquaintance of mine used to begin conversations, whenever two or more women were gathered, with the question, "Guess what Dinko did?" The first time I heard her say this so contemptuously it took me a moment to realize that she was

referring to her husband. Needless to say, theirs
was not a model marriage. But over the years, the
phrase has become a joke between my husband and
me, a question we ask with glee whenever one of us
does something stupid.

So, guess what Dinko did? I'll tell you.

My husband often travels to Sacramento for his
work. He likes to take the train so that, thanks to
the wonders of technology, he can work on his lap-
top computer while he travels. (He can also watch
DVDs with it when he gets tired of working.)
Traveling by train is an ideal arrangement, much
less stressful than driving. He took the evening
train from Bakersfield a few weeks ago, but not long
after he departed, I got a slightly frantic phone call.
It seems that, when he went to use the tiny hard
drive containing his work files that he keeps on his
key chain, he realized that he did not have his car
keys. Now, one does not need car keys to travel by
train. But he was pretty sure he had left his keys in
plain sight on the driver's seat of his car, which was
now parked for three days and nights at the train
station. He had already imagined the scenario
wherein a shifty-eyed thief, while strolling through

the parking lot, sees his keys, smashes the car window, and steals his car. So he was calling to ask me to skip the dance class to which I was headed, drive from Tehachapi to Bakersfield with his spare key, retrieve his keys, drive back home, and then drive the keys back down to him when his train returned in three days. I told him I considered this a *big* favor. A HUGE favor.

But, since I really do love him and promised I would forever, I did it.

My sense of superior intelligence was short-lived, however, as one weekend it was my turn to do a stupid thing. Guess what I, the Dinko, did? I'll tell you. Reluctantly.

We decided to hike a six-and-a-half-mile portion of the Pacific Crest Trail through Cameron Canyon, outside of Tehachapi. We both like to hike, and we thought it would be a good way to spend some quality time as a couple, which we had been thinking lately we don't do enough of. So we packed our water and apples and trail mix bars, put on our boots, and set out on a lovely morning. We parked my car at one end of the trail, and then drove my husband's car to the other end. The plan was to begin our hike at his car's end, end it at mine, drive back to retrieve his car, and then go home. Not a very ecologically sound way to hike, I admit, but we were just trying to establish this new, healthy habit, the logistics of which were a little complicated.

The hike went swimmingly. We talked exhaustively, touching on things we don't get around to in the course of a normal busy day; dreams and philosophy and life's conundrums. We took pictures, admired the last of the wildflowers, and worked up an honest sweat. We ate our snacks, drank almost all our water, and were hot and grubby by the time we came over the last crest and saw my car, ready for our return home.

It was at precisely that moment that I realized that my car key was safely stowed in my purse, locked in the trunk of my husband's car. That's right: six-and-a-half-miles away. "You didn't happen to bring the extra key to my car, did you?" I ventured, my heart sinking, not relishing the role of Dinko.

He had not. He had only his car key, the key to the car he drove. He naively imagined that I would have the key to my car, the car I drove.

The thought of the return hike was daunting, to say the least. Another three hours, on very little water, on growling stomachs, on tired legs, on sunburned necks? I had really done it this time. I wondered how long it would take our children to miss us. I wondered if they would ever find our bones.

Fortunately, my husband (motto: *Be prepared with as many technological devices as possible*) had brought his cell phone, which I (motto: *Carry as little as possible, as even one key will slow you down*) had not. So we were able to call a very kind and understanding friend, who drove to where we were stranded. He picked us up and took us back to my husband's car. He and my husband had a good laugh over my keylessness.

As have pretty much all of my husband's friends, one of whom has sweetly given me a magnetic hide-a-key. Yeah, very funny.

"At least you'll never do that again," said my husband, and I hope he's right. I hate being the Dinko.

My husband and I decided we were even, trading train station fiasco for hiking disaster. We're a good, albeit car-key-challenged, match. We may have to start carrying our car keys around our necks.

The moral of these tales of misadventure in Dinkoland, in case you were wondering, is that a workable marriage is one of give and take. Of giving each other good stories to tell at work the next day. Of taking turns being the idiot. And of never, ever, referring to each other in the presence of a third party as "Dinko."

reflections . . .

What does my partner see in me? What do I see in my partner? Really see? And really love? The unaccountable, intangible ties that bind us are also the colorful threads of our particular experience of intimacy.

If we are indeed from different planets, Mars or Venus or the disenfranchised Pluto, where in the heavens do we meet? Perhaps we can be more sensitive to our differences as we strive to find ways to keep our interplanetary relationship viable. May we live long and prosper!

Am I comfortable being the Dinko sometimes, or do I always need to be the superior being, the one who looks down on the Dinko? Are my partner and I able to be vulnerable in each other's presence? Or are we merciless? A great gift, both to give and to be given, is to be able to be wrong and still feel loved and valued.

$\mathcal{K}$-i-s-s-i-n-g

Rejoicing in each other, they returned to their
   bed,
   the old familiar place they loved so well. . . .
But the royal couple, once they'd reveled in all
   the longed-for joys of love, reveled in each
   other's stories.

HOMER ON ODYSSEUS'S REUNION WITH HIS WIFE PENELOPE,
THE ODYSSEY

My face in thine eye, thine in mine appears,
And true plain hearts do in the faces rest.

JOHN DONNE,
"THE GOOD-MORROW"

A Little Cello Music

My husband is taking cello lessons. He practices a scale, up and down, and the sound swells the house. It is not yet melodious—more like a mama grizzly in labor or a headache that has not quite visited the temples. At best the low notes rattle on the breastbone like a horror movie soundtrack— impending doom, close-up on the victim's hand reaching for the knob: *Don't open that door!* Our children shut their bedroom doors. Our dog scratches at the back door for mercy.

The cello itself is a thing of beauty, despite the unlikely growls coming from it. Its polished wooden curves glow in the lamplight. It nestles between my husband's legs, a lovely place to be, and he draws the bow across its strings smoothly, caressingly, his

19

ear bent to hear the notes. He looks peaceful,
though he makes an occasional sound—whether of
dismay or satisfaction, I cannot tell.

And as crazy as it is—he doesn't have the time,
we don't have the money, he's a grown man for
God's sake—I love him for this. I love him for
bringing this enormous instrument into the house
and driving us all to distraction. I love him because
he looks at a cello and is not daunted.

My husband has always been willing to try new
things. It is a quality that often led him to grief in
his adolescence but that serves him well as an
adult. In his teaching career, he is a groundbreaker,
a forward-thinker. As a father, he is a first-rate
adventurer, building doll houses from scratch and
trying out new recipes and scaling ever-higher
heights of computer literacy with our children.
And as much as our children roll their eyes at the
introduction of this velvety-throated stranger in
the large zippered case, they are taking it in. They
see that a person is never too old to grow.

Deep in his heart, my husband has always
wanted to play the cello. He has music in his soul.
When I first met him, he was never without his

harmonica. He carried it the way some men carry a pocket knife, ready with some blues for any situation. Music of all kinds has always filled our house; the radio is always on in the car. He has taught our children to play the recorder and has made up songs with goofy lyrics for them since their births. He lucked out onto a cello teacher, complete with an instrument to loan, while setting up a music program for his school. A boyhood dream was by chance fulfilled, the important lesson being that his dream was still accessible to his everyday consciousness. Mine are not so close to the surface.

So often we parents teach our children the defeats and surrenders of adulthood. We tell them how we could have been contenders—if only, if only. We urge them to learn from our mistakes even though we don't. Reach for the stars, we say, as our hands dangle earthward. Never stop trying, never stop dreaming, we say. But if we ourselves, in little things and large, no longer try or dream, then that is what we truly teach.

That is why I love my husband so, as the squawks and grunts emanate like digestive problems from his cello, as he squints at the music on the stand as he plays his piece. All the tired lessons, like practice makes perfect, and try, try again, and the one about the new leaf—all spring to life as he embodies them for us, he and his blessed, bellowing cello. He's almost got "Moon River" down.

By Christmas I expect we will hum along to bass-clef carols. As we all know, angels sometimes sing with the most unlikely voices.

Rocks of Ages

> Trust in the Lord forever,
> for in the Lord God
> you have an everlasting rock.
>
> ISAIAH 26:4

My husband and I have taken up hiking as a way to spend time together, to stay connected as a couple, and to preserve our bones into old age. My husband is a long-distance cyclist, and I am not. I like to tap dance, and he does not. Hiking is our compromise activity, our meeting of the muscles halfway.

In honor of my husband's birthday, we hiked a trail along the northern Kern River, in Central California. The river was swift, beautiful, and treacherous, home to kayakers and white water rafters, deadly to casual swimmers. It commanded respect. It cascaded into rapids and falls, and tumbled over and through massive rock formations. As we hiked single file along the narrow path, and listened to the pounding rush of the river, we conversed little. For several miles, we were companionably lost to our own thoughts. I thought about the patience of nature through the centuries, relentlessly and imperturbably going about its work. And I thought about rocks.

I don't know much about rocks. I remember learning in school the different types: igneous, metamorphic, and sedimentary. Being a literary rather than a scientific person, I liked the sounds and meanings of the words, but retained very little of the geological information.

Rocks are our connection to the beginning of time, and will remain here long after us to root another future in the past. We are the fossils of tomorrow, clambering over the essence of the earth's crust. There is a mystical permanence to rock. It is no accident that the steadfastness of advertised entities is compared to the Rock of Gibraltar, no accident that St. Peter was called "the

Rock." Although the rocks had likely moved and shifted, tumbled and split through the centuries, I imagined Native Americans on those exact Kern River rocks.

Other elements of the landscape bent and changed direction to accommodate the rocks. Trees grew in curves and angles, seeking precious light around the rocks. Plants sprouted from infinite crevices, their roots adapting to unforgiving soil. Even the river, whose power had smoothed and contoured the rocks over time, seemed to flow around some of the immense formations in its bed.

As immutable as the shapes of the rocks appeared, their colors changed with the light of the sun, reflecting the Creator's palette that we call earth tones. The progression of the hours on the water and the rocks made the hike out look like it followed a different path from the hike in.

We agreed it was a day from God.

I think of those rocks, anchored and unyielding and strong, seemingly eternal, when I am back to my routine of daily life, on my husband's un-birthdays. I am still drawn to the rocks, down to my cells and molecules. My modern life is full of the temporary, things that are disposable, things that don't last. We move houses, change jobs, change cars, change hair colors, seeking what is better and new. So much is done in passing, in transit, a quick and patchy fix that doesn't solve a deep problem.

But the rocks abide, steady, constant, true. Jesus tells us at the conclusion of his teachings in the Sermon on the Mount, "Everyone then who hears these words of mine and acts on them will be like a wise man who built his house on rock" (Mt 7:24).

To hear and to act. Jesus tells us exactly how to find that solid ground, that solidarity with his people, that rock-solid faith. On a fall weekend, the earthly rocks of the Kern River reminded me of ancient wisdom, of enduring patience, of unfailing love, of God.

Who, if we listen, even speaks to us on birthday hikes.

Dance (Life) Lessons

My husband cheated this past Christmas. Let me hasten to add: in a good way. Every year we agree on an amount that we are going to spend on gifts for each other. I bought one gift for him, the thing he really wanted. With tax, the price came to five dollars over my limit, so I suppose in a way I cheated first. I confessed immediately. He just smiled.

On Christmas morning, he gave me an array of lovely things. He liked his one thing. But then he told me that he had arranged, as an astonishing gift, for us to take dance lessons together. We were going to learn to swing dance in time for the annual Valentine dance at our church. I happened to see the check he wrote to our instructor. He went way over budget.

And I love him for it.

Dancing has been a part of my life as far back as I can remember, even to when I was a left-handed preschooler and began every shuffle-step in tap class on the wrong foot, much to my teacher's dismay. Years of dance have taught me to be right footed. I danced through high school and college, reveling in ballet, tap, modern, and jazz. The unkind years since have left me more suited to yoga, and to contemplating the Zen of aging. But I still love to dance.

All of my daughters have traveled in and out of dance classes with varying degrees of commitment.

When one of my daughters earned her first pair of pointe shoes, I could have cried over how beautiful they were. My daughter was amazed that I, a decidedly non-sewing mom, knew exactly how to sew on those long pink satin ribbons. But some things stay with you always.

My husband, on the other hand, has always been a reluctant dancer, an obligatory wedding dancer, a slow-dance dancer. He has been known to invent some wacky dances with the kids, but is not keen on performing them in public. He has more talent than his awkward self-image allows. But these lessons were truly a gift from the heart, as I knew they were not within his comfort zone. It also probably didn't help him that in order to get to the dance room we had to cut through a basketball practice where two dads were coaching. Both of whom he knew. And to whom he had to explain what we were doing there. And whose faces took on that falsely sympathetic, better-you-than-me look that men think wives don't notice them exchanging.

Our instructor was a very sweet high school senior who could dance circles around both of us, and whose vast store of patience was older than her eighteen years. In the process of our dance lessons, we learned far more than rock steps and loop turns: We learned about our life together.

The first thing we learned is that I am a control freak. I wanted to lead. In swing dancing the man has all the power. He decides which step is coming next, and sends his partner a signal by how he leads into the step. I found myself anticipating, often not correctly, which way he was going to send me. I had to adapt to the elements of surprise and mystery. This probably speaks volumes about the dynamics of our marriage, but I had to stop myself from analyzing twenty-three years of habit in front of our young dance instructor. Just dance, I thought. Dance and shut up. And it worked! I'm learning to be led to unknown places, at least on the dance floor.

The next thing we learned is that we do not spend enough time together as a couple. We had to move heaven and earth to find one half-hour per week to dance together. We are both so busy and scheduled that we have gone several days without practicing our steps. Which made us realize that we often go several days without transcending the mundane, pass-the-pepper level of communication. We need to make time for each other. We are, deep down, soul-mates, kindred sprits, companions for life. At least now we know that when the kids are grown and the working is finished, we can always put on "In the Mood" and dance.

The last thing we learned is that we want to learn more. At our final lesson, my husband told our wonderful instructor that she could probably go into business selling dance lessons to husbands who want to be romantic. I almost said that I don't know that there are too many like him. But why be cynical? Especially when our plans included future lessons in the foxtrot and the waltz. We are now dancing fools. Our grand goal is the tango. I imagine us, old and wrinkled, dressed for an elegant evening, dramatically stalking across the dance floor, cheek to cheek and heart to heart.

With time and practice, we'll get there. But for now, just jitterbugging hand in hand is a thrilling gift.

reflections . . .

Do my spouse and I value learning? What new thing have I tried in the past year? Anything? To say that one is never too old to learn something new is a long way to express one magnificent human word: hope. Old dogs can learn new tricks, provided they are willing to think like a puppy again.

What rocks do we rely on as a couple? What rocks are we willing to scale together? What keeps us climbing? Identifying the anchoring rocks in our lives, as well as the boulders that block our way, can keep us on solid marital ground.

Do we dance together? Is one of us willing to extend a hand to the other in invitation to the dance? Is it always the same one of us? It is important to take turns leading in the dance of life, and to stay on beat.

30

First Comes Love

Love is composed of a single soul inhabiting two bodies.

ARISTOTLE

You can't blame gravity for falling in love.

ALBERT EINSTEIN

Exactly What Is Intimacy?

Intimacy has several definitions in *The New Oxford American Dictionary*: "close familiarity or friendship; closeness . . . a private, cozy atmosphere . . . an intimate act, esp. sexual intercourse . . . a closeness of observation or knowledge of a subject . . . "

Well, yes. All of the above. We'll take one of each.

Intimacy with our mate is as close a familiarity as we can have with another human being, in that we share everything—from a mortgage to parental responsibilities to bodily fluids to a tube of toothpaste. Intimacy can be a cozy atmosphere, a private club, or it can be a conflagration of emotion, a public nuisance. Our intimacy involves sexual intercourse, as well as every other kind of intercourse.

We will never be as closely observed by or obser-
vant of another person as we are with our spouse.
We are a living record of each other: our triumphs,
our fears, our history, our hopes, our aging, our
growth. Intimacy can be as reassuring as it can be
terrifying.

Intimacy is necessary to healthy human development and to a life of joy. Everyone needs to feel
that there is someone to count on, to lean on, to
share a joke or a hug or a particular misery; someone who knows the best and the worst in us and
loves us anyway; someone whose presence is both
comforting and energizing. We are blessed by God
to find the specific person on earth whom Anne of
Green Gables called a "bosom friend," the person
with whom one bares one's inmost soul. And while
single, celibate people hopefully form those especially close relationships in community or family,
happily married people are fortunate to live each
moment of life in an especially intense intimacy.
While I do not mean to ignore the many enriching
intimacies among people of all walks (indeed, in
my informal polls among friends on the topic of
intimacy, many cherished relationships involved

neither vows nor sex), it is on marital intimacy that this book concentrates, as that is the focus of the author's vocation, if not exactly expertise.

Sometimes we can define a concept more helpfully by determining what it is not. Marital intimacy is not equal to proximity or familiarity. Plenty of couples stick out a marriage for the sake of the kids or finances or health insurance or appearances or just plain inertia and are miserably lacking in intimacy. They may sleep in the same bed and share the salt and pepper shakers until one of them dies, but they are not necessarily growing in intimacy. They may be lifelong roommates, but they are not soul-mates.

Nor is marital intimacy exactly equal to honesty. Or at least not the kind of mean-spiritedness that masquerades as honesty, as when a personal attack ends in, "Well, I'm just being honest." Honesty matters, of course. Honesty is huge. But brutal honesty—the kind that tells me that my butt really does look big in this dress—is not always called for in wedded intimacy. Sometimes we really do need our mate to be a dry-eyed realist, but sometimes we need our mate to color in the harsh outline of reality with the pastels of love. True intimacy involves knowing the difference.

Marital intimacy is emphatically not equal to sex. Anyone can have sex, for any number of reasons. Casual sex, sex like in the movies, neither springs from nor enhances intimacy. Having sex can, strangely enough, be an incredibly lonely experience, and I'm not even taking the Internet into account. The physical act of sex can be devoid of meaning and feeling. Sex can be had with a stranger or for a fee. It can be numbing or humiliating or clinical or single-mindedly orgasmic. Sex, the closest physical thing you can do with another human being, is not necessarily intimate.

But when it is, it is sublime.

We live in a society that advertises that sex should be had as early in adolescence and as frequently as possible, that the best sex is spontaneous and responsibility-free, that virginity is a goofy, unrealistic notion, and that premarital sex is a smart way to find out if a couple is sexually compatible.

In reality, the excitement and novelty at the start of a sexual relationship are hardly indicative of lifelong compatibility or intimacy. A marriage is not well grounded on a fortuitous orgasm. Ideally, a marriage is based on love, respect, honesty, trust, friendship, communication, romance, mutual goals, faith, and true enjoyment of each other's existence. These qualities in a relationship give birth to sexual compatibility. Sex in this context becomes increasingly intimate, knowledgeable, and fulfilling over time. With no false luster to wear off, a couple learns together to shine with true light.

I think it is important, especially for Catholics who are sometimes obsessed with guilt (and with the sneaking suspicion that something that feels this good must be bad), to recognize and affirm that marital sexual intimacy is good. It is, in fact, great. It is worth the trouble. Sexual intimacy between two people who are committed to each other and to God for life is a transcendent experience. It is a sacramental experience. In spite of the confirmed celibate St. Paul's backhanded and begrudging nod—"I wish that all were as I myself am. . . . But if they are not practicing self-control, they should marry. For it is better to marry than to be aflame with passion" (1 Cor 7:7,9)—it's okay for us married people to have sex. (And most advisable *also* to be "aflame with passion.") Sex is how we produce all those new Catholics. It is also hot, satisfying, and the most fun of all earthly pleasures. Sex is how we connect, how we unwind, how we relate, how we cherish, how we commune, how we express what we cannot always say. Marital sex may not always be candlelit or per- fectly choreographed or perfumed. But it comes from a deep and abiding love, an almost unbearable closeness that mirrors God's love for us. It is good. And, it *matters.*

If it didn't, why would we spend so much time wanting it, thinking about it, worrying about it, reg- ulating it, justifying it, counseling it, fixing it, pret- tying it up? We yearn for sexual communion with our spouse. We yearn for intimacy, even as it fright- ens us to be so completely vulnerable to another person. We know the potential for damage and hurt and destruction. But we want it anyway. We want to believe that two people can strip down to their very souls before each other and survive. And thrive. We want to experience total trust in another because that is our holy design. We have faith that it can be done. We have seen it work in others, in ways that prove the existence of a loving God.

❧

As an apple tree among the trees of the wood,
    so is my beloved among young men.
With great delight I sat in his shadow,
    and his fruit was sweet to my taste.
He brought me to the banqueting house,
    and his intention toward me was love.
Sustain me with raisins
    refresh me with apples;
      for I am faint with love.

THE BRIDE, SONG OF SOLOMON 2:3–5

You are stately as a palm tree,
    and your breasts are like its clusters.
I say I will climb the palm tree
    and lay hold of its branches.

THE BRIDEGROOM, SONG OF SOLOMON 7:7–8

I am my beloved's
    and his desire is for me. . . .
Let us go out early to the vineyards,
    and see whether the vines have budded,
    whether the grape blossoms have opened
    and the pomegranates are in bloom.
There I will give you my love.

THE BRIDE, SONG OF SOLOMON 7:10–12

We sometimes pretend that the Song of Solomon, or the Song of Songs, is a metaphor for the spiritual love between God and his chosen people in the Hebrew Scriptures. But seriously, it reads more like foreplay. Anyone who knows what it is like to be "faint with love" recognizes the juicy imagery of sex in the quoted sections above: "Sustain me with raisins," indeed. We know the urge to "climb the palm tree" ("I say I *will!*") and the feeling when "the grape blossoms have opened." These are words of desire, of passion, of release. They are not words for which we need to make excuses. Romantic human love is a towering component of marital intimacy, even if it is not traditionally viewed as a higher calling.

There are many rooms in the marital house of intimacy: physical, sexual, intellectual, emotional, cultural, and spiritual. When we marry, we exchange the keys to each room along with our vows. In each room, we give and we take. We welcome and we entertain. We accept and we respect and we love whatever is inside. Each room is essential to the integrity of the house and functions in its own unique way. We may not always clean up after ourselves. We may have a favorite room. We may redecorate. We may lock the door behind us. But we definitely live there.

When my husband and I were newlyweds, we made a disastrous decision and moved into an old house with another married couple whom we had recently met. We thought we'd save a lot of rent money and gave no thought to the loss of our privacy. We signed a lease for one year. This might have worked if the house had more than one bathroom. But after one month, a year had never seemed so long. Small annoyances grew huge. For example, the other husband was a large man who took long baths and then sprinkled himself liberally with baby powder. The slippery powdery floor became a point of conflict for us, and many more altercations followed: the way we cooked, the way we cleaned, the hours we kept, the friends we entertained, the way our cats fought, the way *their* cat once used *our* bed as a litter box! We finally managed to break the lease and move to separate places. We suffered five months of close-quartered misery together. In retrospect, I think the forced intimacy of the situation— sharing in the personal moments and odd habits of

people among whom no natural intimacy previously existed—doomed the arrangement from the
start. Intimacy follows love and affection and
respect. It cannot come first. It cannot be imposed.
It cannot be faked.

In the Mood

The wonderful documentary *Mad Hot Ballroom*
chronicles a ballroom dancing program for fifth
graders in New York City. The ten-week program,
called "Dancing Classrooms," was started ten years
ago by the nonprofit organization American
Ballroom Theater. Students learn to perform five
types of dance: merengue, rumba, tango, foxtrot,
and swing. The movie follows the metamorphosis
of these boys and girls into the "ladies and gentle-
men" that their dance instructors call them. The
program culminates in a city-wide competition that
keeps the audience both smiling and on the edge of
their seats.

The movie contains interviews with the students as they become dancers and learn to interact
with their partners on such a stylized level. One
girl discusses her goals for her future and then

comments on how dancing relates to real-life relationships. "Oh, I'm not in the mood for boys right
now," she says matter-of-factly.

Not in the mood for boys. What a delightful statement for her mother to hear! I found myself hoping
her mother appreciated this attention to studies
and extracurricular activities before boys, because
it is a sentiment I have never heard from the lips of
my youngest daughter, and I know I never will.

Not that my daughter has always been boy-
crazy, which I point out hastily, lest I get into a lot
of trouble at home. When she was just beginning
ninth grade, she was a steady and balanced
student. But for some reason, I noticed that her
class as a whole, ever since about the fourth grade,
had been obsessed with pairing off with each other.
The girls in her class had always been in the mood
for boys, and vice versa.

"I'm going with Ebenezer" *(not the boy's real
name),* my daughter would announce, at the age
of ten.

"You're not going anywhere with Ebenezer,"
I'd say. "You're ten years old."

"Mom," she'd say in an exasperated, adult tone.
"I mean we're going out."

"No, you're not," I'd say.

"Well, he's my boyfriend. And Maggie's going with Brick, and Eleanor's going with Franklin, and Ginger is going with Fred." *(Again: not their real names.)*

Two days later, when I'd ask her how Ebenezer was doing, she'd respond with disdain, "We broke up. I'm going with Abraham L. now." And all of the previously mentioned couples would also have broken up. Fred would be with Maggie, Eleanor would be with Brick. It was either a mess or a very intricate dance.

The revolving-door relationships among she and her friends continued through the sixth grade, by which time she had gone with just about every boy in her grade, even though she had never actually gone anywhere with any of them. It was some sort of ritual, that every girl be paired up with a boy. And they never even learned any ballroom dancing.

I was briefly concerned when I heard her, at the age of ten, discussing how Fred had cheated on Maggie with Eleanor. Cheated? This sounded serious. How exactly, I finally had to ask, does a ten year old cheat?

"He talked to her at recess!" she said indignantly. "In private!"

I was relieved that cheating didn't involve anything overtly physical: No one was making out behind the portable classrooms or groping each other in the library. I could just hear her answer if I were to voice these concerns: "Oh, *gross*, Mom!"

My two older girls, themselves being what one might call "late bloomers," used to enjoy their youngest sister's status reports on who was going with whom on what day. They were convinced that the baby of the family had already had more boyfriends than all the rest of her sisters, and they wondered when elementary school had become *Peyton Place*. Or, to use contemporary terms, *One Tree Hill*.

As a high school junior, my youngest daughter recently had a boyfriend (of course), who was a nice young man. But they still didn't go anywhere alone together. That's because we, her parents, are impossibly strict, uptight, humorless people who have no idea what it's like to be in high school, and who persist in dressing in ways that are meant solely to embarrass her in public. But before we know it, she will be allowed to date for real, and she will gradually become, as have her sisters before her, more woman than girl.

It will be interesting to see the pairing-off future of the class of 2009, if they marry more quickly than their generation now does, if their passion for going with each other translates into adult commitment at younger ages. I hope it does not translate into a long, long list of temporary partners or into searching for their own identities only through the eyes and approval of others. I hope they can dance on their own two feet before taking on more complicated steps. We shall see what the future brings. Time, as we older folks know, can do amazing things.

As my girls grow up and fall in love, I am always tempted to borrow a line from the 1950s-era mother in the movie *Peggy Sue Got Married*: "Peggy, you know what a penis is? Stay away from it!" Especially when they're in the mood for boys. Boys, I want to tell them, are *always* in the mood for girls. But it is not fair for us mothers of daughters to cast all boys in the role of the devil: Any tango, after all, takes two. I have to trust that my daughters have been raised to care about themselves and others, and to think independently, and to behave with grace. I have to have a little faith in them and then get out of the way.

Single Summer

A few years ago, my husband was gone for eight weeks of summer, participating in a fundraising bicycle ride across America. As he biked the days away from Seattle, Washington, to Washington, DC, I was temporarily the single parent of four daughters. It felt like forever—the longest summer of my life, even longer than the lonely stretch between seventh and eighth grade, when I knew I would start school as the dorky new kid from another state. Now I had more to miss.

My retired neighbor Frank was living the single life, too, while his wife tended to a sick aunt in Tennessee. He told me what he missed: "She left me meals in the freezer, but it's just not the same as her at the stove cooking them. It doesn't smell right." Temporary singleness was a stomach thing. For Frank, food. For me, a shriveled feeling in my depths. I missed my husband even more than when he was my college love, finishing his degree in a different state as we planned our wedding long-distance. I missed him dramatically then. Now I just ached quietly.

Because, of course, there were the children, who missed their father. I watched other dads at the pool, rough-housing, throwing their kids in the water, and I realized how necessary that was. I didn't do that. There was a definite, pronounced absence in our house. I thanked my lucky stars that it was not due to death or divorce, but it was still off-center. There was more than rough-housing for them to miss: stories in a scary voice, a hug against a strong flat chest and a stubbled chin. Height. The secure smell of testosterone. Math riddles. A second opinion. Salsa that's too spicy for anyone else. A game of UNO. Ginseng tea brewing in the morning.

I had several friends who were single moms, whom I had always felt were noble and brave to face parenthood alone. But they had, one by one, let me in on a secret: Single motherhood isn't so bad. "You'll love it," one friend told me. "It's just you to deal with—you make all the decisions. It's sort of peaceful. No compromising and all that." This was a friend who was married, tried that two-parent thing, and preferred going it alone. She relished her parental independence. She didn't worry that the house wasn't clean or that a well-rounded meal wasn't hot and ready when he came in the door. "It's much easier," she said. "Much more relaxed. You'll see."

Another formerly married friend agreed. "I did miss my ex when he was out of town, back when I still liked him," she said. "But you'll do a lot less picking up when he's gone."

Okay, so she was right about that. The house did stay neater with my husband gone. There was a certain serenity to going about my daily business, even as I felt like I was doing time. And we had some goofy meals—like pancakes in front of the TV, a usually forbidden activity. I found myself falling into a not unpleasant autocratic rhythm, as my single friends told me I would. But as my orderly side took over, I realized how much my husband balanced me. At night everything was pristinely in its place, and I had to face the realization that I was a borderline anal-retentive personality because he was not there to render neatness impossible or silly or unimportant. I had a sobering vision of myself had I remained single—one of those women in a big denim dress, frighteningly organized, empowered by my roar, setting out the night before the chunky turquoise jewelry I will wear in the morning, when I will sweep my intentions over my coworkers. I felt all yin, no yang.

And let's face it—I could fix my toilet, clear my weeds, have my oil changed, capture spiders, barbecue, and take on all the usual dad tasks. But when the kids were asleep and the chores were done and the dogs had been let out and I had read several chapters of the new Walter Mosley novel, there was the bed. That was the loneliest time, as the lamp on his side remained unlit, and the bed was far too wide. Even if my husband and I just had a heart-to-heart over the phone from Idaho or wherever, there was one thing we really did need men for. Or my particular man, who knows me inside out, body and soul. By the light of the moon we transcended the merely physical to celebrate our oneness. There was no replacing, no substituting, no sublimating that. In spite of attempting solidarity with my single friends, I realized men were not expendable after all.

During the day I could be confident, capable, bright, in control, hardworking, and loving. I have the best kids in the world, and spending time with them was a joy and a privilege. They tracked their dad's progress on a big map of the USA, taking turns drawing each day's line of a hundred or so miles. They kept a journal of our daily events for him, recording everything from a pair of busted shoes to the fireworks on the Fourth of July to a nerve-racking visit from a rattlesnake. I was eternally blessed to watch them grow in strength, independence, and beauty.

And yet, and yet, there remained a sweet hollowness at my core. I half-enjoyed watermelon, the sunset, a good movie, a walk in the morning, a new shirt, a new idea—half. The other half of me was preoccupied, far away, one day in Missoula, Montana, a few weeks later in New Ulm, Minnesota, even though I'd never been to those places. "Sideways," my husband called it. He felt it, too.

Maybe every marriage needs a fundraising bike ride at one point to make the partners realize just what it is they love and appreciate in each other. But a shorter ride. Say, San Francisco to Los

Angeles. I knew I would be the happiest woman alive when my husband reached the National Mall in Washington, DC, thus signaling the end of my single summer and our long-distance intimacy.

At least Frank's wife had come home, and as I saw the pride and contentment on his face as he watched her sing in the church choir, I knew all was right in their world. She was back to fill his stomach with fragrant home cooking and his days and nights with companionship and love. We should all be so lucky.

reflections . . .

Are my spouse and I intimate, or are we inti-mate strangers? Do we share the keys to those rooms of physical, sexual, intellectual, emotion-al, cultural, and spiritual intimacy, or do we lock each other out of one or more of them? I have to be willing to fling open the doors and raise high the windows for my beloved to enter fully and intimately.

Am I a kind, giving, and sympathetic partner, even when I am not "in the mood for boys"? Do I persist in the action of loving even when I may not feel particularly "in love"? The words of love are nowhere near as important as the deeds of love.

Do I ache when my spouse is not present? Do I feel completed by my spouse? Or are we losing something precious? Help is available, both pro-fessional and divine, and we would do well to ask for it if we need it.

53

Then Comes Marriage

He's more myself than I am. Whatever our souls are made of, his and mine are the same.

CATHERINE SPEAKING OF HEATHCLIFF,
WUTHERING HEIGHTS BY EMILY BRONTE

It's having that trust with another person that you can show him the silly you or the dark side of you and he is still going to like you.

MY SISTER KYLE
SPEAKING OF HER HUSBAND OF FOUR YEARS, VINCE

Doing It (What Comes Naturally)

If you've been married for any length of time, you could probably write your own book on intimacy. You have your own fat album of wedding photos, your own troupe of children, your own family stories and inside jokes, your own blessings and sorrows, and through it all, your own life partner. You are indeed doing it already.

If you have teenagers, you may be snickering at the title of this section: "She said *doing it*." As laudable as it is that you are so tuned in to your teenagers, we need to examine carefully our impulse to snigger at things that make us uncomfortable. Things like talking about sex. About the birds and the bees and Cole Porter's educated fleas. About doing it.

We don't often hear homilies dealing with marital intimacy, even though marriage and family are
integral to the structure of the Church, let alone the
raison d'être for the local parish. The Church wants
married couples to do it, of course, so that the
human race will continue to journey on the path to
salvation. The Church just doesn't really want to
talk about it. And it definitely doesn't want to hear
about it. Married people have long been the silent,
apologetic majority of Catholics. They are not in
positions of leadership. They are not living the
vocations of which we are regularly encouraged to
pray for more. They are not beatified unless they
have committed their marriage, strangely enough,
to celibacy. Those who do it have traditionally been
second-class holy people, tainted by a necessary
and better-left-unmentioned earthliness. So how
do we married folks, within our parishes, share
and communicate and learn and pass on our
vocation, about that to which we are called, and all
that we know is right and good?

We offer engaged couples the experience of
classes, or weekend encounters, before they are
married, when all the information is still a bit theo-
retical. We get them talking about marriage as a

sacrament, about decisions they will face as a couple, about potential areas of conflict, which is all good. But once they are living it, where is their supportive faith community? I know there are parishes with excellent outreach programs to the married, but I have never lived within the boundaries of one. There are marriage encounter weekends as well, which my husband and I have long had good intentions of attending, but haven't gotten around to doing yet. We rarely come across a free weekend on our family calendar. We also rarely have an extra nickel. If you are married, this may sound vaguely familiar. The years fly by.

But every time we take in a movie or go for a walk together or have friends over for no special reason, we are deepening our intimacy. We are indeed doing it already, every time we breathe a prayer together or rejoice together or grieve together, every time we give our partner what he or she needs—even if we don't understand it. Every time we have coffee or snuggle or laugh or make love, we become more intimately intertwined.

Once we are married, it goes without saying that we are doing it. Or does it? The media has pelted us with an arsenal of articles on "sexless marriages," which apparently are marriages in which the partners have sex fewer than ten times a year. On top of worrying whether we are doing it right, we must now also worry about whether we are doing it frequently enough. The average married couple, we are told, has sex once or twice a week (even as we are also fed the exaggerated claim that men think about sex every *seven seconds*). We try to observe our marriage with clinical eyes. Are we normal? Are we sexless? Or are we, heaven forbid, *oversexed*?

True marital intimacy has nothing to do with frequency, and still less to do with averages. Or with what is considered normal. Most people I know are right-handed, but the fact that I am left-handed does not indicate that there is something wrong with me. We are people of foibles and failings and idiosyncrasies, as well as people of gifts and blessings and pearls of beauty. When we come together, all of those intricate and bizarre qualities come with us. They make us who we are and, ultimately, lovable to the one who loves us most. Our sexual intimacy is unique to our marriage. Hence, how or when or where we make love is all secondary to whether we are in communion when we make love: the why.

The blood went bounding along his veins; and the thoughts went rioting through his brain, proud, joyful, tender, valorous.

She was walking on before him so lightly and so erect that he longed to run after her noiselessly, catch her by the shoulders and say something foolish and affectionate into her ear. . . .

A wave of yet more tender joy escaped from his heart and went coursing in warm flood along his arteries. Like the tender fire of stars, moments of their life together, that no one knew of or would ever know of, broke upon and illumined his memory. He longed to recall to her those moments, to make her forget the years of their dull existence together and remember only their moments of ecstasy. For the years, he felt, had not quenched his soul or hers.

JAMES JOYCE,
"THE DEAD"

There is nothing lukewarm about intimacy. It is an extreme state: We never modify the adjective "intimate" with "sort of," just as we are never "sort of" in love. While we may be sort of hungry or sort of apprehensive, we are never sort of intimate with another person.

Our mates are lights to us: "the tender fire of the stars." Ideally, our mates not only balance us, but teach us how to be our best selves and then make us want to be better. The daily details of our marriages may seem tedious or unchanging, especially during the years of raising young children. But if our eyes remain open, we can count on flashes from above, holy moments of true love, when we glimpse God in the way our hearts leap at our lover's touch, or at the sight of our beloved's leg muscles in motion, or the sound of a laugh, or the whiff of a body that smells like no other, or a hundred other images that may course "in warm flood" along our arteries.

Marital intimacy is an incarnate love, a reflection of God's love shown in the gift of the incarnate Son.

The Magic Touch

At age nine I had an epiphany. I was watching my parents hold hands as we walked across a parking lot after a football game. It was late afternoon, and they were in front of me, their silhouettes tilted toward each other intimately. It was a jolt: the first time I perceived them as something separate from me. They were my parents, but they were also a couple, a man and a woman who had fallen in love and whose happiness was captured in those black-and-white wedding photos and who still loved each other enough to want to hold hands on an autumn afternoon.

Now I am the mother, and I've been caught.

"Close your eyes," says my eleven year old to her older sister. "Mom and Dad are kissing in the kitchen again." She giggles.

"Get a room," says our fourteen year old, seeing how far she can go before she shocks us into disciplinary measures.

But they are used to seeing us kiss. I believe it's healthy for parents to kiss in front of their children. It's good for them, like fresh air and oranges and clean clothes. It helps them grow in tender and nurturing ways.

As much as I think of us as a couple in love, albeit four daughters later, those same children see us as their parents first. It doesn't always register that we also interact as man and woman. I know our two older children's initial reaction to learning how babies are made was to picture Mom and Dad doing such a ludicrous thing and then to say, "No way! Not my parents!" (Or, as a friend's child said with a sweet smile upon learning the mechanics of reproduction: "I think I'll adopt.") Now as teenagers I imagine they are faintly repulsed at the whole idea of their parents as romantic creatures. Our youngest, when she was in middle school, on the cusp of many things, regarded us thoughtfully as she worked things out.

Our children have never caught us in the act, I'm happy to say. There was one close call years ago, when just as we were catching our breath, a light shone in our eyes. It was the beam of a circus flashlight, a gift that day from Grandpa, followed by a weaving, half-asleep child, making her way to our bedroom. No police spotlight could ever seem brighter than that flashlight did to us. After that, we locked our bedroom door. Although it's possible that our children have heard us making love, we take precautions. We check on young sleepers. We say goodnight to teenagers holed up in their rooms, music safely blaring. We close our curtains, light the candles, check the door lock again, and attack each other.

In some ways we are like wayward teenagers ourselves, sneaking around, having surreptitious sex, giddily celebrating the rarely empty house. But while our lovemaking is discreet (except for the very occasional stolen quickie in the garage), our physical affection for each other is not. Our children have grown up with the awareness that we dig each other.

Married sex continually delights with its intimacy, its innovation, its deepening appreciation for the physical gift of each other. It becomes more pleasurable with time, trust, and love. It's easy to buy into the advertising line that sex is for the young and beautiful. But the better portion secretly belongs to us: the faithfully married, even with our deepening lines and softer bellies, our visible veins and the gray threads in our hair. Yes, there are dry spells, when life is so busy we fall into bed exhausted. We don't have time for sex, as it's not on the to-do list. But sooner or later it makes its way to the top of the list, as we drop everything and feast on each other. Then we realize why we've been so grumpy lately. "Why don't we do this more often?" we ask each other. It is a question with no good answer.

We are touchers. We are huggers. We hold hands when we walk. Our touching is an expanding circle. We snuggle and smooch our kids. Our teenagers can only handle a brief arm around their shoulders without embarrassment. But this parental touch is just as important as inhaling their baby-sweet necks used to be. A child who is loved and touched affectionately at home is less likely to seek physical gratification elsewhere.

We touch, we love. We have four vivid, beautiful daughters: fruit of the power of this awesome thing we do with God. Are we role models for their future relationships? I hope so. I hope the old adage about looking for someone just like dear-old Dad is not far from the truth. I could wish them no greater joy than the magic of a touchable marriage.

My parents have celebrated their fiftieth wedding anniversary. The waters of joy and sorrow, of success and disappointment, of anger and forgiveness, have flowed mightily under their bridge. Yet along their journey, their touches of love have enthralled, soothed, and healed.

My parents are my daughters' history and roots. My daughters are my parents' hope and affirmation. My daughters think their grandparents are adorable as they share their vitamins at the breakfast table and correct each other's stories of long ago, of the Navy and hard times and their first baby daughter.

I notice they walk more slowly. But they still hold hands.

The Vows That Bind Us

When we decide to marry, we, at some point, become preoccupied with the vows that we will make in the sight of our families, friends, and God.

"I take you . . ." Take you where? Will I have to take you everywhere I go? Will I find your presence suffocating as your face appears at every turn and around every corner in my life? Will I have to surrender my privacy, my inner being, my core self? Am I cut out to be married?

"To be my lawfully wedded husband. . . ." Or will you be, as my uncle used to joke, my *awfully* wedded husband? Under the law, we will be as one. *I fought the law, and the law won.* Do I know you well enough to take you on legally? To marry you? Who are you, anyway?

"To have and to hold, from this day forward, . . ." I like to hold you. I like to be with you and touch you and kiss you and know you are mine. I want to hold your hand and have your babies and tell you I love you every day. I still get butterflies in my stomach when you look at me that way.

"For better or for worse, . . ." Does this mean that you won't always look at me that way? That you are on your best behavior? That the minute we are married you will scratch yourself and drink too much and pass gas publicly? That there will be things I don't like about you and can't change? That we will see each other's warts and flaws? That we will have our tragedies? I want to go back to the butterflies. I want to keep the butterflies!

"For richer, for poorer, . . ." I don't want to be poor! I want to have enough money to pay the bills and have a little fun and, sure, give something to

charity when we can. I want to be able to stay home with my kids if I want. I want to focus on the richer. Please be employable. Be steady. Be financially sound.

"In sickness and in health, . . ." When I am sick, I want my mother. Are you going to want me to be your mother? But we're both pretty healthy. Will one of us be hit with some degenerative disease? Will the other be able to handle it? I know that I will have to become a better, stronger person to deal with anything happening to you.

"Forsaking all others. . . ." What if my perfect mate is still out there, waiting for me to realize the hugeness of the mistake I am making? What if the hot UPS man finally asks me out? What if we are not MFEO? (Made For Each Other, according to the precocious girl in *Sleepless in Seattle*.) What if we bore each other a little more each year until there are only tears?

"I will love you and honor you, . . ." What if you turn out to be neither lovable nor honorable? What if I turn out to be neither lovable nor honorable? Will God still hold us to these promises if they turn out to be foolish and naive?

"All the days of my life." That seems like a really long time. What if we grow apart, become incapacitated, despise each other? Or what if one of us dies too soon, leaving the other to grieve and mourn all that was never ours? If I give you my heart, will you promise you won't die on me?

There is much to fret about here. There is much to fear. But there is also much to expect and much to create. We know, just by agreeing to marry, that there is much to love. There is much that is unknown, and much that is best left in God's hands, which is where we place ourselves when we marry.

And most of us, the ones you don't really hear about, are doing the intimacy thing just fine already. With lots of room to grow.

Be present to each other and experience in the depths the gift of life! Christ didn't fall into solutions or solving problems—that's the temptation of the desert. That's our temptation—to solve people's problems, to cure, not care. To care means being where the suffering is. It's a way of living together so the mystery of life is revealed.

HENRI NOUWEN,
THE ROAD TO PEACE

An intimate relationship is not always rosy, or even comfortable. Some days are hard. Some days are even harder. Some days just need to end so that we can start over. There are days when I indulge in the admittedly sinful fantasy that I live alone. I imagine I am single and childless. Everything in the house is mine, and I know exactly where everything is located because I have placed it all just so, and no one else is around to interfere with my master plan for life. The house is quiet and stays reasonably clean. Every choice—the music that gets played, the television that gets watched, the meals that get eaten, the pictures that get displayed on the walls—is mine. I am organized and frugal and at peace. I do not take myself for granted. I do not treat myself insensitively. I never suffer frustration or burnout or anger.

But every now and then, an evening occurs where everyone in the family has somewhere else to be except for me. Once, this happened for an entire weekend. And after an hour or two, it's awful. I invariably feel incomplete, useless, at loose ends. I suffer from something I usually cannot imagine: loneliness.

My mother told me that she always wanted our house to look like a model home when I was growing up. And indeed, there were rooms into which we did not venture for fear of making an unforgivable mess. But with six children and their various pets and projects and friends, there was little chance of that unlived-in look. Now that we are all grown, my parents' house is perfect. And my mother says she would give up every inch of decorated sterility to go back to the days of spills and stains and the breathless life.

I realize that, like everything else in this earthly life, living in intimacy is a tradeoff. Any bed of roses is also prickly with thorns. Being present to each other in intimacy will definitely involve suffering, but often, if we allow it, it is a shared suffering. And we won't always be able to cure each other, or fix our problems, or build a perfect world for ourselves. But the message of Jesus is that he will always be found in the dark fissures and hollows and low points of our lives and our marriages, offering us a light for our way and teaching us compassion.

Going to the Chapel of Love

Of course it ran through my head all day, on that first Saturday of October:

Going to the chapel and we're
Gonna get ma-a-a-rried.

Even though it was a large Catholic church rather than a chapel, and it was my sister getting married, not me. But what a wedding it was!

It had been many years since our family had enjoyed a wedding, but my sister's made up for the drought. It was a lavish and lovely event. My sister was a stunning bride in a white gown that sparkled with tiny crystals, and her groom cleaned up all right. (Kidding! He was a dashing and handsome figure.) She and her fiancé had invited over two hundred fifty guests, about two hundred of whom actually came. Their meticulous planning spanned most of the year, and no detail was too unimportant to ponder. Their wedding party was the size of some small weddings I have attended, keeping the florist and tuxedo guy and bridesmaid dress shop all in business for another season. Just about every member of our considerable extended family was included in some way, as well as my brother-in-law's family.

A wedding day, in the scheme of normal days, shines like no other. It is like finding the only whole sand dollar on the beach, or wishing on the first evening star as night begins to fall. It is one of those indelible days in the family scrapbook, and for happy reasons. It marks the end of the search for a kindred spirit with whom to spend a life, as well as the breathtaking beginning of that shared life. Even when things go wrong on a wedding day, they are not really wrong. The overall joy of the day glosses over any errant steps. If the music doesn't start on time or the flower girl gets cold feet or the power goes out, it doesn't matter. As long as the bride and groom are willing to commit their two lives to becoming one, the wedding will be remembered for its perfect beauty and hope.

Because what represents human hope more visually than a wedding? Everyone present is there out of love for the bride and groom as they begin their married journey. Among the witnesses, the unmarried dream of what may lie ahead for them just beyond the next crest. The married are walking the path wherever it leads and bends and plunges and climbs. The widowed reflect on the bittersweet and on the end of that well-traveled road. Everyone present is touched.

The priest who presided at my sister's wedding was a friend to both bride and groom. He was a gifted communicator, and as he spoke, he reminded the couple of the examples of marriage in their families and the wisdom therein. But then he sounded the most hopeful note of all, telling them that he prayed that this newly married couple will do better than those who had preceded them. It was a heartfelt point, and one that every parent feels for a child, that we want them to go beyond what we have done, to learn from and perhaps avoid our mistakes and misjudgments. Surely that hope holds true for every infant marriage. When the bride and groom repeat their wedding vows, we secretly wish them more health than sickness, more good times than bad, more light than darkness, all the days of their lives. We wish them a highway long and straight, even though we know in our hearts that it's often the rocks and potholes that form us and draw us closer together.

When my sister and brother-in-law spoke their feelings to each other after their traditional vows, I was grateful for the existence of waterproof mascara. (I cry at all weddings, even fake ones in movies, so I should have been smart enough to pack a hanky for my sister's.) Their faces alight with love and hope, they expressed how happy they were to have found each other and how they had come to be standing before us on this blessed day. They exchanged rings, they kissed, and they left the church as a sacrament in the eyes of God.

As a married woman, I know there will be days when they will want to pinch each other because he didn't change the roll of toilet paper or she didn't tell him about a dinner engagement; when your spouse makes you so mad you could spit. But on this wedding day, standing in the chapel of love, I really only remembered when we once stood in the same spot, making vows we planned to keep and facing the future brightly. I silently renewed my sacred promise from all those years ago. I could say that I envied the newlyweds their youth and unblemished hope. But then I looked at my beloved, and I wouldn't have life any other way, which is the untold joy of somebody else's wedding day.

$\mathcal{P}utting$ the Naked Back in Marriage

When we mix together our busy schedules, four daughters, and an unforgiving budget, my husband and I rarely get away together, as the marriage experts advise. Our vacations are usually visits to friends or relatives, or family camp outs. Our idea of indulgence is take-out Chinese food eaten after the kids are asleep. A play or concert is an extraordinary treat. Even a movie on a big screen happens only on a blue moon.

Of course we love our children. We love being Mom and Dad. But sometimes we love—we need— just to be us. So when my husband got the nod from his school district to attend a weekend conference in Big Bear Lake, California, complete with a private hotel room, we didn't think twice. In our minds we were already there. And naked.

Finally on our way to the conference, our first stop was my parents' house to drop off our children. We unloaded all their clothes and stuffed companions, kissed the kids, wished my folks all the best, and drove through the fog and threatening snow to the mountains.

The hotel room was gorgeous, sumptuous. The bed was topped by a canopy, and sheer foamy fabric draped seductively from the top four corners. A fringed shawl hung above an ornate mirror, and starry curtains framed the window. There was an armoire, a fragile table and two chairs, and an inviting tub. The lamp by the bed was turned down low. The gas fireplace hissed instantly, intimately, at the flick of the switch. We left our bags by the door and melted.

In the morning a whole new world greeted us. Snow hugged the limbs of the pine trees out our window. We were awakened from our cocoon by a telephoned wake-up call instead of by the patter of little feet ready for play or a dog's cold nose. Morning desire needed not be furtive or unsatisfied. We ate bagels and bananas in bed. We showered together. When my husband left for his first scheduled meeting, the day was at my mercy.

Part of me luxuriated: Shall I pull out my unread novel, go for a walk, polish my essay-in-progress, order tea, watch a movie, shop for souvenirs? Part of me panicked: What will I do all day? No plans, no schedule, no car pools, no responsibility, no example to set? What a wild and terrifying prospect for a mother of four on a Saturday morning! What if I make the wrong choices, and later regret my free hours unwisely spent? I watched the fire and decided to find my book. I hung out the "Do Not Disturb" sign, feeling deliciously wicked. I was going to be just fine.

When I met my husband for lunch, we walked arm-in-arm, matching our strides like we used to in college. We still fit perfectly. We ordered lunch, and we talked to each other the whole time. Our conversation dipped below the surface, beneath the house needing painting and our daughter's lost tooth. We talked concepts and dreams. We said things we didn't even know we thought, but which were freed by uninterrupted time. We fell in love.

Our weekend, when not committed to meetings, was devoted to sex. Sex at home was comfortable, fulfilling, warm. Sex in a hotel room was on a steamier level. The kind light of the fireplace meant even I could successfully wear a garter belt. We could make more noise. We could stay naked all the time. And we could be certain that the person in room 225 was not going to have a raptor nightmare and want to curl up on a corner of our bed.

Sex on a stolen weekend was everything you read about and more.

Big Bear Lake? Oh, yes, it was very nice. We ate hearty meals, admired the lake, took in the shopping village, jogged through towering pines. The people were lovely, the conference informative, the parking not bad. But to be honest, a weekend in the Mojave Desert would've probably brought the same light to our eyes.

Sunday always comes. We packed up, checked out, and made our way down the mountain. As wondrous as the weekend had been, as much as I loved the quiet conversation of our driving time, I felt the flutter of anticipation in my belly: the kids. I really had missed them. I wondered how they'd been, if they'd eaten well, if they'd picked up their toys and watched out for each other. I wondered if they'd missed us, but I knew they had. I imagined them flying across the driveway when we pulled up, all tight hugs and wide smiles. They would be taller and brighter, even in two days. We had brought them souvenirs, little bears, and smelly soaps. They would tell us all their high adventures with their grandparents—forty-eight hours worth.

Life would be instantly back to normal as we all came together again.

My husband and I would cherish in our hearts our two days of rejuvenation and refreshment, and exchange private smiles. He still looked great naked.

Ch- Ch-Changes

> Ch-ch-changes / Pretty soon now you're
> gonna get a little older. . . .
>
> DAVID BOWIE

Every year our parish holds a renewal of marriage vows, followed by a dance. A single friend once remarked that it wasn't nice to hold such an exclusionary event: What about the widowed, the divorced, the celibate, the lonely? I understood her point, but I also thought about the way the eyes of all those husbands and wives were shining at Mass, and the way they danced to the love songs so closely afterward. A night like that at the parish may be exclusionary, but a night like that for a marriage is necessary.

We married folk get caught up in the small annoyances, the schedules, the daily compromises, the details of leaky faucets, bad report cards, incontinent dogs, unexpected expenses. In the face of routine and familiarity we must find ways to surprise and delight each other. Every now and then my husband calls me during the day, his office to my office, to say he loves me. On some days, that call makes all the difference.

In the course of a marriage, we change and change again. We lose our wedding-day smoothness. The straight path from the magical honeymoon becomes bumpy or obscured. My shiny golden wedding band has scratches and dings from the hazards of daily wear. My face has creases and sharp angles, smile lines that remain after the smile fades, years of bliss and tragedy etched therein. My aging bones make ominous cracking sounds. It's hard to remember being the buoyant girl in my wedding photos, the girl at whom one day my grandchildren will point and ask, "Who's that?"

Once upon a time, my bridegroom and I dreamed of a life in the theater. We thought children were a long way down the road. We made love every day, sometimes more than once. We saw new movies and read groundbreaking books and attended art exhibits. We smoked cigarettes and shared bottles of wine and did not concern ourselves with our health, or our weight, or our mortality. We worked pizza jobs and janitor jobs and somehow made ends meet with our collective minimum wages, with never a nickel leftover. We didn't think a lot about God. We didn't think we would ever be as old as our parents were then.

We have changed so much. We have become who we are.

We are middle-aged parents who worry, who exercise, who don't smoke or drink, who own a house, who make a good living, who have no idea of what is cool, who pray a lot, who age, who fall into bed tired more often than not. We are older, wiser, more embattled, more careful. And I wouldn't have us any other way, because we are also closer to each other than I would have ever thought possible.

Change is inevitable. Change is our friend. Change pulls us apart. Change is what is left in the back pocket of life. All of these statements are sometimes true. Life can change in a heartbeat, in a glance, in the time it takes for a car to skid or a virus to multiply. Other changes are so gradual as to be imperceptible. As the French say, "The more things change, the more they stay the same." Maybe the French are referring to cycles, to the way history tends to repeat itself, the way we make the same mistakes from which we thought we'd learned our lessons, the way our daughters wear bellbottoms and Dr. Scholl's sandals.

The only thing that doesn't change is change itself.

Our marital roles have undergone changes, as well. We who began as bride and groom became ardent lovers, and in time the parents of a young family. We have been coaches, chauffeurs, nurses, tutors, fans, driving instructors, disciplinarians, bankers, and ready ears. We are now somebody's folks at college orientation, seasoned lovers, kindred spirits, intimate friends. I remember watching my husband sleep with our firstborn baby snuggled on his chest and marveling. He changed diapers. He took over the clipping of tiny crescent fingernails, of which I had a pathological fear. He was the storyteller, the pied piper, the monster in the closet.

As he changed into a father, I fell in love with him all over again. I imagine that someday I'll be falling in love with somebody's grandfather.

A lasting marriage needs to be able to change course, to flow freely, to go with an unforeseen bend in life's river, to take on the rapids and float in the calm shallows. In other words, we need to have faith. When this does not happen smoothly, we are in conflict. When this is not an organic process, our marriage falters and chugs into hurtful waters. When we are unbending, unyielding, we break. The ability to change is often what keeps us from bogging down, as is the ability to surprise.

That is why I tell my single friend that we need to indulge in those cherished evenings of marriage vow renewal at our parish. We need to rediscover the deep and sometimes buried roots of our attraction. We need to celebrate romantic love. It is, after all, our calling. We get to see that our marriage has turned out to be a pretty good partnership so far: not without change, not without concession, not without strife, not without countless blessings. If a marriage reflects Christ's relationship with his Church, therein lies a tale.

Your faithful love in a marriage and family is tested by change. It can also be strengthened and brought to maturity through change. The challenge is to remain open to the Lord's gracious, healing presence and to see change as an opportunity for growth.

U.S. CATHOLIC BISHOPS,
"FOLLOW THE WAY OF LOVE"

reflections . . .

Do we leave room in our marriage for our sexual selves? Do we give and respond to that Magic Touch? While there are plenty of times when we are truly spent by the course of the day, we nourish our marriage by embracing the intimacy of the night.

Do my spouse and I inhabit our vows? Do we walk the talk? Do we even remember what we said on that lovely, lacy, long-ago day in the church? We know in our hearts that we would do it all over again: Let's take a moment to say so!

Am I, like Adam, ashamed of my nakedness? Am I able to appear naked in the eyes of God, to bare my body and soul? If not, am I open to change? I can't avoid change forever, even though that's the plan I might prefer.

CHAPTER FIVE

Then Comes a Baby in a Baby Carriage

I asked him with my eyes to ask again yes and then he asked me would I yes to say yes my mountain flower and first I put my arms around him yes and drew him down to me so he could feel my breasts all perfume yes and his heart was going like mad and yes I said yes I will Yes.

MOLLY BLOOM'S SOLILOQUY,
ULYSSES BY JAMES JOYCE

It is only with the heart that one can see rightly; what is essential is invisible to the eye.

ANTOINE DE SAINT-EXUPERY,
THE LITTLE PRINCE

Authentic married love is caught up into divine love and is directed and enriched by the redemptive power of Christ and the salvific action of the church, with the result that the spouses are led to God and are helped and strengthened in their lofty roles as fathers and mothers.

SECOND VATICAN COUNCIL,
PASTORAL CONSTITUTION ON THE CHURCH IN THE MODERN WORLD

We mostly don't think of our parental roles as "lofty." Parenting usually seems much grittier: Ever had a day with an infant when milky vomit and poop that squirts like French's mustard have taken turns spewing from this little being onto your clothes and person until you reek? Or picked splinters out of overly adventurous toddling feet? Or hosed beach sand from every crevice of a little

kid? Or laundered fully ripened PE clothes? Or figured out if it's worth letting the insurance compa-
ny know about the body damage your teenager
"kind of" inflicted on the car? Right: lofty stuff.

But we can get a bit lost if we think of the
things of God as lofty and the things of life as somehow separate. We sometimes keep God in that ded-
icated space in our brains reserved for memorized
prayers and religious rules. We don't invite God
out to go bowling. We invoke God in times of trouble and tragedy and thank God for times of great
joy, but perhaps we err in thinking that God has
more to do than pay attention to the less glorious
parts of our lives and that prayer exists on a higher,
more *spiritual* level of reality.

The fact that God participates in our boring
days is what makes even the smallest thing we do
lofty. The fact that we trust God and attempt to
bring the love of God into all of our relationships,
the fact that God is present in the messy and the
mundane, in the *details*, the fact that God cannot,
after all, be kept on the special top shelf: These all
guide our married love toward authenticity. God
helps and strengthens us parents—the weary, the

sticky, the broke, the confused, the unfashionably dressed, the blessed, the lofty.

The Family Bed

> We'll be together with a roof right over our
> heads;
> We'll share the shelter of my single bed
>
> BOB MARLEY,
> "IS THIS LOVE?"

What a relief—Dr. Richard Ferber, that famous expert on infant sleep, as well as an advocate of the hideous practice of letting babies cry themselves to sleep, has relaxed his ban on babies sleeping in their parents' bed. I guess it's okay to come out now. We confess: We slept in a family bed. Parents in much of the rest of the world regularly sleep with their babies, but American experts have long frowned on the practice. Apparently, though, co-sleeping is on the rise in America.

My husband and I began our marriage with a double bed. Actually, it was a futon on the floor. Hey, it was 1980. We were young and flexible. We moved a lot. Not owning a box spring and head-board helped more than it hurt.

When we had our first daughter, we planned to tuck her into a hand-me-down cradle that we had lovingly sanded and repainted. But when she arrived home, she spent little time in it because whenever we put her there she woke up and cried. If you are a parent, you know the scenario: The sweet infant is finally asleep. So is your arm. You are wearier than you thought possible. You carefully, carefully, lower the baby into her baby bed. You move by centimeters, freezing when the baby squirms. When she is again calm, you resume the descent into slumber. The baby is in contact with the mattress. So far, so good. She is still sleeping. Your mind is hovering invitingly on the joys that await: two free arms, a shower, a bit of adult time, sleep. You slowly extricate your arm from under the baby. The baby sighs, and settles. You cover her with her baby blanket. You tiptoe toward the door. Life is good. It's about to get better. You can feel your back beginning to unkink, your neck relaxing, your mind returning from lullaby lyrics. But just as you turn to shut the bedroom door, you hear her stir (oh, no . . .), and fuss (ohh, noo), and cry (OH, NO, NO!). You want to cry along with her. Maybe you do. You have a momentary flash of understanding for the perpetrators of shaken baby syndrome. Then, hugely ashamed, you begin the dance of baby sleep again.

If only the baby would stay asleep!

Our family bed was born of futility rather than philosophy. The first time our daughter slept with us, it was accidental. Up again in the middle of a freezing night, I brought her under the covers of our bed just to stay warm while I was nursing her. I fell asleep. We both slept until morning for the first time since her birth. Even though I was refreshed, I felt guilty. The parenting manuals admonished against bringing the baby in bed with the parents. It was dangerous! It was the end of your sex life! It would turn your child into a clingy, dependent monster! Maybe it was even kinky!

But sleeping felt so good that the next night, when she woke up hungry and crying, I tucked her into bed with us again. We slept undisturbed. The closeness and connection felt right. I began to suspect that the real aberration was insisting that our baby sleep alone in a different bed in a different room. Co-sleeping was a natural fit for us, all the way through our metamorphosis into a family of six. It may not be for everyone. But the following are some refutations of the arguments against family beds:

It's dangerous: The dangers are if your baby falls out of bed from a great height, or gets trapped in loose-fitting bedding or soft pillows, or if you are so drunk or drugged that you roll on top of the baby and do not wake up when the baby tries to let you know that you are smothering her. As our futon was already on the floor, we did not worry about the hazard of falling. Other families we've known have constructed elaborate siding for higher beds or have moved a crib flush with the side of the bed and then used one side of the crib as protection. We were careful to use bedding that fit snugly and to keep pillows away. I am known to sleep like the dead, but as soon as a baby stirred next to me, I woke up. I am not known for my drug or alcohol use.

It's the end of your sex life: Apparently it was not, as we managed to have three more children. We actually had a modified family bed in that our children went to sleep in their own beds and then joined us in our bed if they woke in the middle of the night. So we shared quality romantic time in our bed before any visitors arrived. But all parents know that once there are children in the house, whether they are in your bed or not, parental love-making must become creative, and often silent and stolen, or perish. Also, there are other rooms in the house.

It will turn your child into a clingy, dependent monster: I can report that our daughters are now independent, non-monstrous young women who did outgrow their need to snuggle with us. As much as I sometimes miss the sound of little feet and the feel of a small flannel-covered body slipping into our bed, I am proud that our daughters are neither clingy nor dependent. In fact, there are times I'm pretty sure that our youngest wishes we would find another planet to inhabit.

It's kinky: No, it's not. That argument is simply mean-spirited.

We graduated to a king-size futon when we had our third child so my husband would not wake up on the floor. But the days of our family bed are long gone. Several years ago, we came full circle by going back to a double bed, which proved to be much smaller than my husband remembered. We compromised with a queen bed: big enough to throw elbows, small enough to spoon.

When we remember the nights of lovely comfort and peace with our now scattered daughters, we would do it all over again.

Thanks for the belated permission, Dr. Ferber.

The Church of Cheerios

My husband pointed to something on the church floor: a lone Cheerio. I looked back at him, and his eyes held mine a moment. Then we smiled. A river of communication flowed between us, between the *Kyrie* and the *Gloria*. I knew his thought, prompted by the leftover Cheerio from the previous Mass: Remember when we used to come to Mass armed with toys, books, little bags of Cheerios—*anything* that might keep the children quiet?

I glanced down the pew at them then: four daughters in various poses of reverence and tolerance, the oldest sixteen and licensed to drive a car, the youngest eight and proud to have made her First Communion the day before. That day was the first time she would come forward to receive the eucharist with us and not have to fold her arms in a "W" and be blessed. I felt a pang of longing for the babies they once were. At the same time, I was delighted and awed by who they are. It's hard to remember the days of Cheerios. I don't recall how to change a diaper. I can't imagine nursing discreetly. I haven't chased a toddler bent on reaching the altar in many years. I actually hear the homily now. I concentrate on the liturgy. What a relief to be past the days of Cheerios.

I am stung to think how quickly I have forgotten those Masses. I have become one of the intolerant pillars of the Church. I sometimes feel annoyed by the sound of a whining child or an unhappy baby in the back of the Church. I think, Why don't they take that kid to the nursery? But it wasn't that many years ago that people were giving me the evil eye if I didn't immediately leave the pew when a baby fussed. Then I would think, Hey, this is her Church, too! I may not focus on a word of this homily, but I am doing God's will! But I still felt guilty for having brought the little yapper to this holy place.

And then I would bring out the baggie of Cheerios, saving the most effective solution for last.

Cheerios are the perfect church food. They aren't sticky and they don't crumble, so they're easy to clean up. Babies like them, and the hole in the middle means less likelihood of your baby choking on one during the consecration. They do have sugar, but they do not have preservatives, so you don't feel too negligent for feeding them to your precious child. They don't smell. They don't roll very far. They don't make noise. They are the Catholic parent's joy and refuge.

And yet, *The New York Times* News Service recently reported that the vice chancellor for the Archdiocese of Chicago finds it troubling that little bags of cereal are sometimes left in the pews. "When you're trying to reach a state of spiritual contemplation," she says, "there is nothing like sitting on a bag of Cheerios to throw you off."

I do understand that it is thoughtless and irreverent for people to leave their trash in the pews. But I think this statement reflects a basic trouble in the American Catholic Church. While we pay lip service to responsible procreation and family values and all that, we would really rather not have to put up with the little howlers that are the tangible breathing results of holy matrimony. Especially during Mass.

I have been to churches with those abhorrent crying rooms, the social equivalent of the hunchback's bell tower. Parents are shown that while their donations are welcome, their participation in the Mass is not. Instead they are provided with a soundproof booth where the entire family can be seen and not heard. It is a miserable environment in which to celebrate the Sunday liturgy: Have you ever seen anyone smiling in a crying room?

I have been in churches where the children are sent packing for the liturgy of the word. In effect, we are telling children that this part of the Mass is really boring unless we dumb it down for you. Rather than learn to participate in the Mass with your family, we think you're better off coloring in a far-off, soundproof room with a bunch of other kids who also don't get it.

Parents have told me that they dread bringing their children to Mass because they are unruly or rude or bored. But these are often the parents who have not brought their children to Mass until they *have* to, which is when they have received their First Communion. It is as though they are saying that with the reception of the sacrament of the eucharist, the jury is back with a conviction: Now the kid has to start doing hard time.

And sadly, parents have told me that they've decided to attend a different church, a more child-friendly church, where they simply feel welcome.

We need to be supportive of young families, rather than treat them as obnoxious burdens that we contemplatives put up with. I remember being the mother with the inquisitive child whom I knew the others in my pew wished I would just take out-side, even though it was snowing. I have sympa-thized with the father whose child sang out lustily, "Ding Dong, the witch is dead!" when the bells rang during the eucharistic prayer. I have, in fact, prayed that the priest would choose the second eucharistic prayer because it is the shortest and therefore the most squirm resistant. And truly, there are extreme times when you do need to remove your child from church. But mostly, young children who are brought to Mass from the cradle, and whose questions are engaged as they grow, learn to be enthusiastic liturgical participants.

As communities, we need to celebrate the essential contributions of families with young children in our parishes. Right now we are very good at making them feel like they are disturbing us, the holy worshipers, who somehow have more of a right to occupy this sacred space. We are very good at making them stay away from Sunday Mass in droves.

We need to welcome our children with open arms, as Christ does. We all belong at the eucharistic celebration, which is, after all, a meal. We eat and drink together. We even do the dishes. My youngest daughter now comes to the table of the Lord with us, but I have to remember that it wasn't that long ago when she was considered a problem parishioner. As for those littlest Catholics in the pews who make such a joyful noise as they shout to the Lord, who says we can't serve them Cheerios at the feast?

Jigsaw Therapy

It is winter, the cold, empty aftermath of Christmas and New Year's, still long before any warm hope of spring. The snow is not as white. The mittens are not really waterproof. The wind is at war with forward progress. It is too cold.

Yet the fire crackles on, inviting as ever. And even if we have no electricity, even if we have run out of powdered cocoa to swirl into hot milk, there is still cause for celebration. It is a snow day. The roads are so icily treacherous that school is closed, which means we get to stay, safe and snug, at home.

But no TV? No stereo, no lights? None of that matters because we have, virginal in its still-wrapped box, a new jigsaw puzzle. One thousand pieces. A lush rain forest scene with exotic foliage and lizards. We can hardly wait to dive in.

But there is jigsaw protocol to follow.

First, the picture has to be one we can all stand to look at. This one is excellent, chosen unanimously at the zoo gift shop last summer. We were thinking ahead. We can't work a puzzle that is nauseating (playful kitties with ribbons) or boring (lobster boats). We also don't want one that is insurmountable: all white, say, or five thousand pieces. We must satisfy a wide range of ages.

This lovely puzzle says everything in French as well as English. "Casse-tete," it says, under the words "jigsaw puzzle," which my college French roughly translates as "head-breaker." We can't wait to break our heads, poetically speaking.

The second important point is to start the puzzle on a big-enough board (there is some math involved), one that can be moved around the house. If we start on the kitchen table and don't finish it by dinnertime, the day's effort has to be stuffed heartbreakingly back into the box before dinner can be served. But the board can go from table to floor to couch, with care.

Dinner brings up the third rule: On puzzle-days, make soup. Minimum-attention soup. Throw all the vegetables you've got in a pot, trust in God, and let it simmer. Add some of the spices that usually stay in the back of the cabinet just for aroma. Stir whenever your legs are stiff from puzzling too long. Serve with all the odd crackers you've accumulated: a jigsaw dinner.

The last, most essential rule: Let everyone work the puzzle however they want. Some like to start with all the flat edges, which are easily identifiable. Others like to pick one flamboyant part to put together themselves—the red bird, or the patch of poppies, or the eyes. Fitting the last piece into a particular section is a good, finished feeling. It is comparable to closing the book on a trilogy or signing your tax return.

The therapy of the jigsaw day is this: Puzzles bring families together. While it is simplistic to encourage counselors to send every family home with a jigsaw puzzle, a puzzle is the perfect indoor family activity. It requires your brains and your fingers, but not the kind of concentration that excludes socializing. You can talk while you puzzle, and sometimes the lack of eye contact coupled with the closeness of faces can encourage surprisingly frank communication. But you can't eat while you puzzle. Greasy smears or wet dribbles on the pieces are forbidden. A puzzle will never go right to your hips.

The act of puzzling can illuminate the lovely variety of personality traits within a family. A child with the ability to think spatially is able to visualize the whole puzzle from its scattered and disjointed pieces: a future architect. A child who begins gamely but is soon bored: a lifelong innovator. One who cannot bear puzzle silence may well be gathering and testing material for stand-up comedy. A child who is blissful in the puzzle's moment: a contemplative in the making. A family may well be an organic jigsaw puzzle—however unlikely the pieces appear, they do all fit.

But don't be like me. Don't become puzzle-obsessed. Long after the rest of the family is over it, I am still trying to fit like pieces with like, shape to shape, color to color. I can't stop. It becomes a mission. While others relax with the puzzle, I must break my head clean in half. I am often the one who finishes the puzzle, in a silent house, late at night, my fingers gritty from the slivery jigsaw dust in the bottom of the box. In the morning, it looks like the puzzle fairy has visited.

So this winter, if you are blessed with an unexpected holiday, rejoice! Let it snow, let the fragrant soup permeate the house, let the candles be lit. Find the puzzle of the *Sound of Music* meadow that a coworker gave you long ago and crack it open.

Gather your loved ones, head to head. Begin to puzzle. You are not wasting time; you are communing. Be grateful for jigsaw therapy, for days like these.

An Audience of One

We recently had the outside of our house painted. It badly needed to soak in some stain and protection. The weather was warm and welcoming, and the windows were open on the side of the house where the two painters were not working. I was at home with one of my daughters while the painters worked, available to answer any of their questions and to offer iced tea. Otherwise we tried to keep out of their way.

As I went about my day, however, I was conscious of being on my best behavior. I spoke to my daughter calmly and sweetly. I offered her opportunities for interesting and stimulating conversation, rather than an afternoon of music videos. With a smile on my face, I helped her bake banana bread. I was a model mother. And all because I never knew when I might have an audience, when one of the painters might need to use the bathroom or let in the dog. I knew the sound of my voice and activities carried through the open windows. I didn't want to be caught yelling or loafing or being anything less than perfect. My image was at stake. I was relieved when the house was finished and I could go back to feeling normal. Not that I am normally a shrew, but I have my moments.

I remember a night several years back when we had friends over to dinner. They stayed late, enjoying tea and conversation, and as the night sky descended I had to give our youngest daughter her bath. I remember then catching myself being falsely lovely. It was a fun bath, full of laughter and discovery, a perfect performance, because I knew our guests could overhear me. I did not yell when my little darling splashed me. I paid careful attention to her requests. I did not scrub her head by rote, my mind elsewhere, without really seeing or hearing her. It was a bath a perfect mom, a mom from the movies or a mom who is really an angel, might give.

But not one that I normally gave.

All it takes is a potential audience to make me choose my words with care, to treat my children respectfully, to craft my appearance. More than once have I spoken sharply to one of my children in the grocery store only to be embarrassed by the presence of another shopper down the aisle whom I had not seen. I seem to save my nicest self for the eyes of strangers. Only those with whom I am most intimate see the real me; the indifferent, perfunctory me.

What I forget, and must realize time and again, is that I always have an audience. God sees me. God is at my shoulder, whether I behave like Mr. Rogers or lose my temper and speak too abruptly. God is watching, whether I take the time to plant spring bulbs with my children or ignore a third request for help with homework. God sees me at my best and at my worst. What a fine mother I would be if I carried in my heart always this piercing awareness of the divine, this intimacy with God.

If I can rise to the occasion with a command performance of motherhood for housepainters and friends, surely that same energy, that commitment and purity, is the least I should give God. But often I settle for the comfortable. I force God into the back row of the theater of life, behind a lot of other less important guests and priorities. "Live as if you were to die tomorrow," exhorted Gandhi, but usually I don't. I figure today is only a dress rehearsal. I assume there will be another day to fix what I let go wrong today, to commit myself more strongly to what matters, to perform more beautifully. So far, I've been right. But what about that last day?

When I was a child, I found the concept of a watchful God more frightening than reassuring, as I imagined that God was looking for fault, for something to condemn. And while there may very well be a divine scorecard with my name on it, I feel the presence of God differently as I grow older. Because I have faltered and failed so many times, and yet each day God is still there, asking me to be mindful as I try again. God is watching, but with eyes of love, an audience of one. The One who knows me best.

reflections . . .

Do we value our children as people, as beings apart from us, as souls? Do we feel that our children enhance our intimacy or encumber it? Do we warm them with inclusion in our intimacy or leave them in the cold? As soon as we birth our children, we begin to give them away to God and to the world. But before they go, our job is to provide them with the tools to build relationships and morals and goals and lives.

Do my spouse and I nurture and tend to our family? Are we good gardeners? Are our darling plantings flourishing and greening? Do they get enough light and water and fertilizer? Sometimes all the garden needs is more time.

If God is my "audience of one," am I going to win a divine Tony? Am I getting a standing ovation after each performance? As a friend once wisely observed about the mystery of life, "This ain't no dress rehearsal. . . ."

CHAPTER SIX

Growing Instructions

Grow old along with me!
The best is yet to be.
The last of life, for which the first is made.

ROBERT BROWNING

A successful marriage is an edifice that must
be rebuilt every day.

ANDRÉ MAUROIS

A Fruit Salad of the Spirit

> Ask anyone who's been married for more than two days about using the fruits of the Spirit.
>
> Most Reverend John T. Steinbock, Bishop of Fresno,
to Confirmation candidates, May 2003

As spring warms to summer, strawberries are on their way out of season, cantaloupe is on sale, cherries are just being picked, watermelon is around the corner, and I'm so annoyed with my husband that I could spit! My hands are feeling melons in the produce department, searching for soft spots, but my mind is on an argument we had this morning, which now seems a long time ago. The day is winding down as I join other tired women in the checkout line, all with quick-fix dinners in their baskets and perhaps unkind words on their minds, too.

The substance of our argument was light—an unmade phone call. The heaviness rested in our tones of voice, our choices of words, our avoided eyes. And while I am holding on to my anger, I feel a small nudge at my heart. I am buying California fruit, but I am attempting to ignore spiritual fruit.

"The harvest of the Spirit," writes St. Paul to the Galatians, "is love, joy, peace, patience, kindness, goodness, fidelity, gentleness, and self-control" (5:22–23). How easily I forget these qualities when it is far more important that I be right. Yet nowhere on the list of the fruits of the Spirit do I find correctness. Or self-righteousness. Or inflexibility. All of which I am seeing in myself as I turn the words of our argument over in my mind. My words lie heavy as rocks and, when turned with honesty, reveal unpleasant slimy creatures hiding in their weighted shade: the destroyers of the Spirit.

The truth is that marriage can be darn hard work. It is a vocation of two. We expect people with other types of vocations, such as priests and nuns, to dedicate their lives to the maintenance and growth of that vocation—that's what they signed on for—but we are sometimes surprised by and unprepared for the work of a marriage. It is not glimpsed in the happy-ever-aftering with which we feed our romantic imaginations. There are those days when it seems like being single would be so much easier.

On the surface we view marriage as a one-time sacrament, like confirmation or baptism: You get to celebrate it, complete with a certificate of proof, once. We treasure the glossy photos, the packed-away dress, the small appliances and place settings of china, the honeymoon memories. It was a day of froth and delirium and dancing and wide-open hearts. Yet, in reality, if this crazy scheme of two-becoming-one is going to work, the sacrament of marriage must function more like the eucharist, in which we are encouraged to participate as often as possible. Daily, even. We must honor each day of a marriage as a sacramental one. On some days we feel flushed with thanksgiving to God for this miraculous spouse. On some days, we praise Jesus for his life-giving example of how to love another.

On other days, we need to get down on our knees and beg the Spirit to sustain us with sweet fruit.

Love. John and Paul (the Beatles, not the saints) remind us in song that all we need is love, and in some ways they are exactly right. Love tops the list of necessary marital qualities. We begin as a couple in love, and while being in love is a heady feeling and makes for a wonderful sex life, it is the self-giving love that keeps us together. Being in love is the "for better" part of the vow. Self-giving love is the "for worse." I remember worrying, after he remained in the operating room during my emergency Cesarean section, that my brave husband would no longer love me in a romantic way after having seen my guts. Literally: The doctor sliced open my ripe belly, lifted up my uterus, extracted our blue (but soon pink) baby, and tucked the uterus back in before stapling me together. This is how my husband later described it. My conscious self was elsewhere. Of course my fear was unfounded, but I think I was really afraid that he would lose that worshipful look that made me giddy in the early days of marriage. While I have since learned that I am not a goddess, I do know that the one true thing I can count on, no matter what, is our love. Even when we are furious with each another, I know that I am the love of his life. As he is mine.

Joy. Surely one of the most awesome joys in a marriage is the birth of a child, and we have been hugely blessed four times over with healthy, beautiful daughters.

It is also one of the most humbling moments to witness what God can create with two people's bodies. We crave these big-ticket joys: Births. The winning lottery ticket. Exotic vacations. The biggest house in the neighborhood. The smartest child. But sometimes I think the Spirit is more likely found in the smaller joys: A light hand in the hair. A knowing glance. An unsolicited word of praise. The physical gift of self, again and again. And even smaller: shared ice cream, a good movie, a walk in the first snow. The joys of marriage are endless if one only has eyes to see. In a stable marriage they are also very much taken for granted.

Peace. "Peace be with you," says Christ so often in the gospels. Peace has to be more than the absence of war. It is more encompassing than a truce. Marital peace is the result of a conscious decision not to strike first, and sometimes not even to defend. The just war theory does not apply to marriage: Peace is the only path and the only goal. Skirmishes will happen over territory or responsibility, as well as guerrilla attacks of ill mood. The peace treaty may have to be renegotiated when differences arise, and new terms established by consensus. There is no justification in a marriage for terrorism, although, sadly, I have seen it occur.

Patience. I would prefer not to address this spiritual fruit because I am so glaringly lacking in it.

All right: Patience is a highly desirable quality in a marriage. Let me know where I can buy some in a large value pack. I confess to impatience again and again. I am impatient at long red lights, with wet towels on the bed, when children forget homework, and pretty much with anything that doesn't go as I think it ought. I work on muting my first reaction. My husband, God bless him, has infinite patience.

Kindness. According to the song, "You always hurt the one you love, the one you wouldn't hurt at all." We often accuse our mate of doing for others what he or she would not do for us. But we do it, too. It is easier to say no to the one with whom we are most comfortable, with whom we feel no need to impress or stand on ceremony. Kindness is the fruit we are more likely to extend to strangers than to our own spouses: Sometimes we are cruel just because we can be. At the end of the day we are too tired/drained/spent to be kind. At the end of the day, this is a mistake. Kindness may be the most underrated of gifts that partners bring to a marriage, and the most infrequently bestowed.

Goodness. My husband is the kind of man who carries spiders outside rather than squashing them, who returns incorrect change in his favor, who will drive far out of his way to retrieve a beloved stuffed animal, who will give his last dollar to anyone who asks. He has a basic goodness that shines in him, and that continually manages to bring forth the good that hides in me. Ideally, married people bring out the good in each other. My mother once said, about a relative and his girlfriend, "They are the worst thing that could have happened to each other." I remember being chilled by the thought of manifesting such utter detriment to another. Married people must strive to be the best thing that could ever happen to each other.

Fidelity. More than faithfulness in sexual matters, fidelity speaks to the commitment of husband and wife to their marriage as something organic and precious, a creation greater than the sum of their parts. Fidelity is inextricably tied to the sacramental, to what is holy in the everyday grit. A sense of fidelity to our marriage enables us to weather the mildly irritating and the tragic and to cherish the mildly delightful and the profound. When my husband and I decided to marry, a number of friends advised us against it, seeing only failure in both of our flighty pasts. Partly joking, we decided that divorce would never be an option, just to spite them. The part that was not joking was the unseen birth of our fidelity.

Gentleness. The human heart is a mighty organ in its capacity to love. Yet it can be broken so easily by the one it loves. Marriage places the heart in a position of abject vulnerability: It is held by another, which feels sublime. It beats for another, which is as it should be. But without the gift of gentleness, the heart can be squeezed to death. Those we love have the greatest capacity to rough us up and harm us. I remember my youngest sister, at a tender age, hugging the family dog and telling him, "You're so cute, I'm just gonna have to kill you!" Which makes perfect sense to me. Gentleness is sensing when to stop squeezing. And when to start.

Self-control. This is where I report that my sister did not kill the dog. Self-control is an underutilized gift of the Spirit because we are tempted to figure, "If I can't let go with my spouse, then who with?" The word "control" has negative connotations relationship-wise, and of course no one prays for a controlling spouse. But we may pray for self-control, which is the essence of maturity, even as we love with reckless abandon. Self-control allows selflessness a chance to breathe and relegates selfishness to the past. It is critical to the vocation of marriage that we mutually "put away childish things" (again with thanks to St. Paul) as we grow together and nurture each other. Giving ourselves over to self-control means that sometimes we will give more than we get, and other times we will get more than we give, in the lovely fluidity of marriage. Contrary to popular opinion, marriage is almost never a fifty-fifty proposition. What strong and true relationship is?

St. Paul's naming the fruits of the Spirit is short and sweet, self-explanatory and comforting. They are simple concepts, but sometimes incredibly hard to put into practice consciously. They are the exact opposite of the brawling and selfish way in which we sometimes instinctively want to behave. St. Paul, no stranger himself to contrary behavior, begins the third chapter of this same letter with the words, "You stupid Galatians!" We humans manage to find such petty detours on our faith journeys, such false starts and potholes on the pilgrim road of vocation. Spiritually speaking, we are directionally challenged. But always, the Spirit beckons. I realize, on my drive home, that I am having yet another stupid-Galatians day. When I get home, I will scoop seeds from cantaloupe, slice fragrant strawberries, add all nine fruits of the Spirit, and serve the careful arrangement to my husband. Who deserves all of this and more.

In the God Shell

It is to peace that God has called you. Wife, for all you know, you might save your husband. Husband, for all you know, you might save your wife.

1 Cor 7:15–16

My sister lives by the ocean, so visiting her is always a plum of a vacation. When we visit in the summer we delight in ice cream and cousins, late nights and board games, sunny days and beach picnics, and always the primordial comfort and deeply satisfying presence of the sea.

I live in the mountains at a high elevation, so it is a special treat to go for a morning run at sea level. It may be psychosomatic, but when I run by the ocean, my lungs breathe more deeply, my legs are stronger, my pace keeps a soothing rhythm with the waves, and I am happy to be alive. And while I pass the occasional dead bird or tossed bag of chips or scattered broken shells, the beach in the early hours is mostly free of clutter. The sand gives a little beneath my feet; the air smells of salt and eternity. A run on a flat beach allows your mind to wander. It begs you to think, to expand, to philosophize.

I ran this morning thinking about my twin nephews turning ten, the occasion of this visit. Ten years ago, they were a difficult surprise, eight weeks early, angry monkey-like preemies in incubators. Now they are sturdy boys of ten, offering no physical reminder of their dramatic struggle for life: twin miracles of God, and science saved them.

I seldom stop on the beach for shells, but two small perfect ones in my path caught my eye. They were both whole, a rarity for this beach. They were almost mates, but of slightly different designs, rather like my fraternal nephews. I continued to run with them in my hands, imprinting them into my palms, feeling how one was slightly rounder. Then, a bit further on, an even greater prize: a huge clam shell, empty of its clam but perfectly formed and beautiful. I saved them all.

Now they sit on the dresser, the two small ones nestled into the hollow of the largest. I am visiting my sister this week without my husband, who was too busy to take time off from work. We have spent a lot of time apart lately, both occupied with different projects, especially as he finishes work on his doctorate. As we approach another wedding anniversary, I feel our physical separation deeply, and not without guilt.

I am thinking about our marriage and about God. I have been wanting us to pray more as a couple, more spontaneously than at Mass or before meals. I am unsure how to fit this into our hectic lives, or even how to bring the subject up without my husband thinking I am a holy roller. He made a comment recently about our divergent spiritual paths, about us being at different levels of development, a concept with which I am uncomfortable. I don't like what he means.

In some ways we are like the two small shells, complete unto ourselves, alike enough to seem to fit together, but not quite a match. But the huge shell is roomy enough for both of them. It is thicker, shinier, sturdier. Call it the God shell. In the God shell, our marriage is sheltered and protected, encompassed, united, and strong, even though we remain individuals. The God shell clues me in to what a marriage should be: a spiritual, yet earthly trinity.

Without God as the third partner, a marriage does not transcend the worldly, the contractual. Without God, marriage has no sacramental unity or eternity. Without God, we are separate, fragile shells that are never quite going to fit and that are ever likely to break into shards.

Within the God shell, the fit no longer matters. We are surrounded and cradled and loved, and free to love each other. We are greater than the sum of us.

Yet we sometimes insist on perceiving our marriage as a duo. We think we're in this together, just the two of us, which is another way of saying we are alone. Why is it so easy to silence God's voice? To still God's hand, to ignore God's presence? Surely we want God. But we don't want to deal with God. We want God on paper. We want God for the rough times. Sometimes God is even useful for hiding behind when things get scary.

But we need an awareness of God's presence always: when we make love, when we horseplay with the kids, when we pop corn or drive to Grandma's, when we attend a violin recital or a graduation. We need God in those furtive moments when we look at each other as though at a stranger and think, "But who *are* you?" And we need God when we grieve, when we fight, when we disappoint.

We'd be crazy to think we could do this marriage business alone.

The shells are dry now. Soon I will bring them home, hundreds of miles from the beach, to the mountains. But if I bury my nose inside, they will still smell like the ocean. I'll show them to my husband. I will kiss him, forgive him, ask his forgiveness. We will crawl into the God shell and lie together, listening to each other's heart. In the remembered rhythm of the tide, in the flesh and blood rhythm of our hearts, God is beating, God is calling, God is loving.

All we need to do is say yes.

*T*wenty-Five Is a Relative Number

In the divine scheme of the universe, twenty-five is not a grand number for anything. Twenty-five miles? Nothing. Twenty-five years? Inconsequential. Twenty-five centuries? A cosmic sneeze.

Within the confines of my earthly life, however, the number twenty-five looms proportionally larger. Twenty-five dollars? A serious chunk of change. Twenty-five pounds? Catastrophic to the girlish figure. Twenty-five years of marriage? A huge amount of time. Twenty-five years equal a quarter of a century, roughly a third of my projected life span.

I remember when my parents celebrated their twenty-fifth wedding anniversary. I thought they were old and hopelessly out of date, like expired yogurt at the back of the fridge. It was 1978, and I was twenty-one years old. Surely that fact alone made them seem old. Their silver anniversary matched the silver in their hair and the tarnish on their antiquated views. Or so I thought.

Because the joke is on me, the years have flown exactly as fast as my parents told me they would and my husband and I now sport the silver in our hair. And the laugh lines on our faces. And the children who think we are antiques from another century.

So we celebrated our silver anniversary by getting away from them.

We escaped to the beautiful central coast of California, and camped at the state beach in Pismo Beach (". . . and all the clams we can eat!" as Bugs Bunny used to say). For four days we forgot about everything but us. We ran on the beach and talked by our campfire and watched the moonlight on the ocean and snuggled in our tent. We walked around several towns and ate delicious vegetarian food at the excellent area restaurants (hold the clams). We drank chai, figured out the solutions to those slightly maddening sudoku number puzzles, and saw a lot of movies. The extended weekend was our idea of paradise.

We got to leave behind our responsibilities because my parents, now working on fifty-five years of marriage and seemingly downright youthful, came to our house and took over our lives for us. Our girls were spoiled by loving grandparents, the dogs were fed, the mail and newspaper were brought in daily, and everything functioned well without us. My mother even wrote our daughters a tardy note when they overslept for school, something I imagine she hasn't done for quite some time. Thanks to my folks, we truly were able to get away from everything.

And what is a romantic getaway but a harking back to that first, all-important married vacation together, the honeymoon? The honeymoon is a magical sendoff for newlyweds as they embark on the intimate journey of marriage. The freshly married couple doesn't know that the itinerary for their wedlock trip may not always be followed as closely as it should and that along their way they may encounter unexpected developments and tortuous detours, unforeseen digressions and frustrating delays. The road followed will probably not be the route that was planned. But when we married couples actually manage to keep traveling together for years on end, even when a new companion or a solo trip might seem an awful lot easier, we have much to celebrate. A short dalliance, a respite from the highway, reminds us of those honeymoon days and nights, when all that mattered was the light of love in each other's eyes and the ardent hopes for the life ahead. And room service. And uninterrupted time. And a successful negligee.

A romantic getaway after twenty-five years of navigating life together lets us pretend that we have no jobs, no bills, no appointments, no obligations, and even for the briefest moment of imagination, no kids. It lets us fall in love all over again. It lets us remember who we are to each other. Of course, we visited the past: What were we doing twenty-five years ago at this moment? We daydreamed about the future: How can we manage to retire on this very beach? All the while, the present relaxed in a hammock in the back of our minds: Should we call home and see how everyone is doing? No worries there: They called us. As is only fair, because we told them to call us for any reason at all.

We are all familiar with that fateful expression, "The honeymoon is over." Twenty-five years ago, when we checked out of our hotel and went to retrieve the car, which we hadn't used for four days, the battery was dead. "The honeymoon's over!" we laughed as we got a jump for our car from a kind stranger. At the end of this trip, as we were getting ready to drive home, my cell phone rang. "Are you sitting down?" asked our newly licensed daughter, as ominous a question as a child could ever ask a parent. "I kind of did a U-turn," she said. "Like, into a fence." In my car. Right. The honeymoon's over, Jack. I just wish the ending didn't always have to be *quite* so abrupt.

But still, it was a glorious trip. We were refreshed, rejuvenated, and relaxed after our time away together. The body shop estimates were forthcoming, the calendar had not erased itself, and our responsibilities and tasks had not been assigned to someone else. But we could handle it because this is the life and the marriage we built together, for better or worse, for richer or poorer, in sickness and in health, until death do us part. The foundation seemed pretty solid. The walls sheltered us. The view was not bad. There were roses to stop and smell. This was where, for twenty-five years and counting, we were so very blessed to live.

I have found the paradox that if I love until it hurts, then there is no hurt, but only more love.

MOTHER TERESA OF CALCUTTA

That man. Honestly.

MY GRANDMA WHEN GRANDPA ENTERTAINED US KIDS BY LAYING HIS ASPARAGUS ON HIS SHOULDERS LIKE EPAULETS AND SALUTING.

My grandma and Mother Teresa had serious wrinkles and serious suffering in common. While Mother Teresa suffered on behalf of others, my grandmother suffered decades of marriage with a man of whom she often did not approve. Deep down, of course, she loved him: They shared a history of epic proportions. But God rest both of these wise old women: I hope they are playing a celestial game of cards and enjoying smooth heavenly complexions. What they both knew in life was that sometimes love hurts. Only when we are able to give love freely, without counting the cost or anticipating payback, do we go beyond the earthbound kind of love that demands reciprocity for all we do.

Selfless love is Catholicism 101. Look at Jesus. Look what he did. While we know we must strive to be Christlike, we all sometimes shift into selfish-love mode, when we think we deserve gratitude and recognition and appreciation for all we do. But again: look at Jesus. As we grow in maturity in our intimate relationships with God and with others, we find selfless love is actually easier and more fulfilling to give. We cross the border from hurt to healing. Paradoxically, when we love without expectations, we are often overwhelmed by the love that returns to us. Selfless love deepens our capacity for intimacy. But most of all, it is one of life's sweetest mysteries.

Intimacy & Celibacy: Unlikely Bedfellows

> In spite of having renounced physical fecundity, the celibate person becomes spiritually fruitful, the father and mother of many.
>
> *FAMILIARIS CONSORTIO*

Intimacy is not a topic that celibate people address easily. Perhaps priests with whom I have broached the topic were leery of my intentions and were not, as they assumed the direction of the conversation, about to be corralled into a discussion of married priests. One priest friend gently took me to task for implying that intimacy without sex was either impossible or a second-class kind of intimacy, and I realized that he was right: I was asking about his version of intimacy as though it were somehow quaint and foreign and utterly different from mine.

Even the opening sentence of the previous paragraph is not fair of me, because intimacy is not a topic that anybody, married or single, addresses easily. My family and friends are used to my being a freelance writer, and to the e-mails I send asking for their opinions on various topics. I usually get a bunch of responses to subjects like blogs or New Year's resolutions, but very few of them actually answered the one asking for their thoughts on intimacy. (Two, to be exact: My sister, also a writer, responded immediately. A couple of old friends sent along an e-mail that they had composed together, offering this thoroughly delightful instance of intimacy: "When we go out to eat, we make sure to get something different, and when we're half finished, we switch plates.")

"You're writing a book about *what*?" one acquaintance asked me when the word got out, as though I were delusional for competing with the sex experts. I hastily explained that I was not trying to become the new Dr. Ruth (or Dr. Phil), but that intimacy can actually be a spiritual endeavor. "Uh-huh," she replied. "Sure it can." Other friends assured me that they were thinking about their experiences of intimacy, they really were, and were they too late to respond, to help with the book?

Still waiting to hear from them.

The most personally meaningful things in life are often the hardest to talk about and share.

We experience intimacy on many levels, and we hold those connections close to our hearts. We are sexually intimate with our spouse, of course, but we can also experience a deep intimacy with our parents, our siblings, our friends, our mentors. We cannot renounce our sexuality, as it is one of the unique components that makes each one of us who we are. But when we are accepting of our sexuality, comfortable in our own skin, whether celibate or married, we find that intimacy needs no overt sexual expression in order to grow and thrive: In the words of *Familiaris Consortio*, we are "spiritually fruitful." One friend spoke of her surprise at the fast and easy intimacy she felt with her spiritual director, which was a relationship she had never sought out before. Interestingly enough, I don't even know if her spiritual director is a man or a woman: It never came up.

All of our intimate relationships prepare us and aid us in our quest for an intimacy that surpasses all others, an intimacy with a God who loves us unreservedly.

∽৩৶

We find rest in those we love, and we provide a resting place in ourselves for those who love us.

ST. BERNARD OF CLAIRVAUX

A resting place is what we all seek at the end of the day, a place of safety and warmth and understanding. It is a trend in popular American culture that we are "cocooning" more: We physically turn our homes into places of refuge. We spend a lot of money on home improvement so that we have professional-quality kitchens, state-of-the-art entertainment systems, home offices wired for computers that allow us to shop and socialize, and designer spas. More of us are figuring out how to telecommute or work from home. If we play our cards right, we may never have to leave our lovely home within the confines of our gated community again!

But that is a false resting place, a temporal solution to a timeless need. The physical place doesn't matter as much as who inhabits it. Strangely, and in contrast to cocooning, according to figures from the 2000 Census, there are now, for the first time, more households in the United States comprised of single adults than of married couples with children. This means that many people are alone at the end of the day. All the cappuccino makers and Jacuzzis in the world cannot substitute for a beloved shoulder on which to lay one's head. In a world where we can purchase a watermelon specially engineered to be big enough for only one, and single slices of pie, we need intimacy with other human beings more than ever.

reflections . . .

If marriage is a fruit salad, do my spouse and I like the same fruit? If we don't, can we eat from the same bowl, sharing what we like and eating all of what the other doesn't like? Sharing a bowl of anything is a small gesture of intimacy, but one we would do well not to take for granted.

Do we celebrate our anniversaries? Really celebrate them? Dance and feast and make merry? Do we invite God? Because God really knows how to party. God is an awesome lover.

Do I cultivate intimate relationships with people to whom I am not married? Do I embrace a lonely world whenever I can? Am I a good companion? Am I mindful that God gives me the gift of holy intimacy every single day? Am I grateful beyond words?

CHAPTER SEVEN

A Prayer Experience

By virtue of the sacramentality of their marriage, spouses are bound to one another in the most profoundly indissoluble manner. Their belonging to each other is the real representation, by means of the sacramental sign, of the very relationship of Christ with the Church.

FAMILIARIS CONSORTIO

My husband and I once retraced the steps we walked when we were courting and were astonished at the long distance we covered without even noticing. Just as we become intimate with someone through these long walks and deep conversations, we become intimate with God in the same way. With God, we call it prayer. A more profound intimacy with God translates into and facilitates a deeper capacity for intimacy with our spouse.

I know that when I neglect my prayer life, my marriage suffers. I become more petty, less centered; less satisfied, more petulant. I lose my perspective: Marriage, rather than "profoundly indissoluble," seems profoundly difficult. Not that my prayer life has ever been exactly *monastic*. The word *scattered* would better describe the seeds of it—a few words from my lips to God's ear here and

there among the dirty socks and carpools and dead-
lines and phone bills, a bit of blessed silence while
walking the dog, grace before meals, and, on a good
day, a stolen half hour for morning Mass. But
prayer makes a huge difference in our intimacy
with God, just as devoting a few daily moments
simply to catching up on each other's lives and
thoughts and battles makes a huge difference in
our intimacy with each other. The more we make
room for each other, the more we also make room
for God. And God always has room for us.

As Catholics, we sometimes feel awkward pray-
ing outside of the formal setting of the Mass. We
may not pray aloud much (or at all) as a couple. We
can be intimidated by the spontaneous prayer that
spouts from the lips of our fundamentalist brothers
and sisters. We like tradition. We like, and tend to
fall back on, the safety of a format. Thus, the following prayer experience is offered as a bridge
from our private pool of prayer to the larger pond
of prayer as a couple. Even if you feel freaked out
when your spouse suggests reading this aloud
together, do it. Just once.

Prayer Note: Although divided into parts for
wife (#1) and husband (#2), any two people or

groups could pray the following together, for as Jesus told us, "where two or three are gathered in my name, I am there among them" (Mt 18:20).

#1: Let us pray together in the name of the Father, and of the Son, and of the Holy Spirit . . .

All: Amen.

#2: According to the Gospel of John, "The Word became flesh, and made his dwelling among us" (Jn 1:14).

#1: Christ be with us.

#2: May our first words in the morning be of love.

#1: Christ within us.

#2: May our words be the mirror of our deeds.

#1: Christ behind us.

#2: May we embrace the mysterious intimacy of the Incarnation.

#1: Christ before us.

#2: May we see the face of our God in each other's faces.

#1: Christ beside us.

#2:   May our fidelity and respect be a sign of God's communion with us.

#1:   Christ to win us.

#2:   May our love for each other bear fruit in this world and the next.

ALL: Christ to comfort and restore us.

#1:   "And the Word became flesh, and made his dwelling among us."

#2:   Christ beneath us.

#1:   May we be air, water, sun, and earth for each other and grow toward God together.

#2:   Christ above us.

#1:   May we find God in the deep breath that centers us in the middle of the day.

#2:   Christ in quiet.

#1:   May our stumbles and our detours bring us back to God's garden path.

#2:   Christ in danger.

#1:   May our last words of the night be of love.

#2:   Christ in the hearts of all who love us.

#1:   May the living, breathing sacrament of our life bring others to the wedding feast of God.

#2:   Christ in the mouth of friend and stranger.

#1:   May our good and gracious God bless us always and hold us close . . .

ALL: Amen.

(With thanks to the Prayer of St. Patrick's Breastplate)

Closing Thoughts

Once I have written what I have written, what have I to ask, what is there left, except that the writings be disposed of according to God's will.

THOMAS MERTON,
JOURNALS, SEPTEMBER 3, 1941

What I have written I have written.

PONTIUS PILATE,
JOHN 19:22

Write what you know.

EVERY GOOD WRITING TEACHER

If we were only allowed to write or talk about the things at which we are perfect, the world would be a silent place. The intimacy I experience on a daily basis is not perfect. If it were, what would I write about? Perfection is not a human quality. We grow because we fail and start over, we apologize and forgive, we miscalculate and misjudge, but through it all, we love. And thanks be to God that there are flashes and glimmers of perfection given to us in the smallest of intimate things: a shared laugh, the electricity of eye contact across a crowded room, that leap of the heart at love's touch. When we are truly intimate, we are kindred spirits with God.

I'm still not an expert. But it's the end of the book, and I'm still married. Thanks be to God.

BIBLIOGRAPHY

Blankenhorn, David, and Dana Mack. *The Book of Marriage*. Grand Rapids, Michigan: Wm. B. Eerdmans Publishing Co, 2001.

Nouwen, Henri. *Lifesigns: Intimacy, Fecundity, and Ecstasy in Christian Perspective*. New York: Doubleday, 1986.

———. *The Road to Peace*. Maryknoll, New York: Orbis Books, 1998.

VALERIE SCHULTZ lives in Tehachapi, California, with her husband. They have four daughters. She is a freelance writer and has written for many publications including *America, Liguorian,* and *The Bakersfield Californian.*

Celebrating the Sacred in life

Through Good Times and Bad
Prayers for a Lifetime Together
Robert M. Hamma and Kathryn A. Schneider

These prayers are written for a variety of experiences from gratitude for thoughtfulness to difficulty with in-laws. They invite you to hearken back to the inspired words of scripture and the sacred actions of your wedding, whether in your first or fiftieth year together.

ISBN: 9781893732988 / 128 pages / $12.95

Prayers for the Domestic Church
A Handbook for Worship in the Home
Edward Hays

This new edition of Edward Hays's most popular book, which includes a new preface by the author, celebrates the "domestic church"—a family worshiping together at home—with a collection of prayers and blessings that remain fresh and creative for today's families.

ISBN: 9780939516797 / 288 pages / $17.95

Live, Laugh, and Be Blessed
Finding Humor and Holiness in Everyday Moments
Anne Bryan Smollin

Anne Bryan Smollin shows us that while difficulty, stress, and sorrow will always be a part of life, a positive attitude—and a healthy dose of good humor—will help us live each moment, both good and bad, more fully.

ISBN: 9781893732988 / 128 pages / $12.95

This Blessed Mess
Finding Hope Amidst Life's Chaos
Patricia H. Livingston

The author reassures us that in the midst of all the "craziness" we can discover the seeds of creativity and hope.

ISBN: 9781893732155 / 144 pages / $14.95

ave maria press®

Available from your bookstore or from
ave maria press / Notre Dame, IN 46556
www.avemariapress.com / Ph: 800-282-1865
A Ministry of the Indiana Province of Holy Cross

Keycode: FD912070000